WAR & PEACE

WAR & PEACE IN IRELAND

Britain and the IRA in the New World Order

Mark Ryan

Pluto Press
LONDON • BOULDER, COLORADO

First published 1994 by Pluto Press
345 Archway Road, London N6 5AA
and 5500 Central Avenue, Boulder, CO 80301, USA

British Library cataloguing in publication data
A catalogue record for this book is available
from the British Library

ISBN 0 7453 0923 2

Library of Congress Cataloging-in-Publication Data
Ryan, Mark, 1960-
  War and peace in Ireland: Britain and the IRA in the new world
 order / Mark Ryan
   p. cm.
  Includes bibliographical references and index
  ISBN 0-7453-0923-2 (cloth)
1. Ireland—Politics and government—1949- 2. Northern Ireland—Politics and
government—1969- 3. Great Britain—Foreign relations—Ireland 4. Ireland—
Foreign relations—Great Britain 5. Violence—Ireland—History—20th century
6. Violence—Northern Ireland 7. Irish question 8. Sinn Fein I. Title.
DA 963.R93 1994   94—8049
941.50824—dc20   CIP

Production by
Junius Publications Ltd
BM JPLtd, London WC1N 3XX

Printed in Finland by WSOY

Contents

Preface

Change, important change, is under way in Northern Ireland. The stalemate that has long passed for the political dispensation in that region is slowly but surely breaking up. The old certainties are gone and the major players know it. Sinn Fein, with the authority of the IRA behind it, has for some time been undertaking serious diplomatic and political initiatives with a view towards negotiating a settlement. The British government has not only engaged in secret dialogue with the republican movement, but has openly declared its readiness to tinker with long-established constitutional arrangements. The Unionists appear bewildered and bereft of their old cohesion.

Is there any real prospect that the sort of changes under discussion will bring peace to Ireland? In truth, despite all the talk of 'peace processes', joint declarations and ceasefires, there is little chance that the conflict is about to fade mercifully away.

There may be a settlement of sorts. It is possible that Sinn Fein may reach some accommodation with the British government. But any such agreement is unlikely to have a major impact on the underlying issues which gave rise to the conflict in the first place and have sustained it for a quarter of a century. Those who urge Gerry Adams and John Major to clinch a deal in the manner of Nelson Mandela and FW De Klerk, or Yasser Arafat and Yitzhak Rabin, would do well to ponder the continuing mayhem in South Africa and the Middle East. The common feature of 'peace processes' today is that they lead to more slaughter not less.

The massacre of more than 50 Palestinians by a right-wing Jewish settler at a mosque in Hebron, in the occupied territories on the West

Bank of the Jordan, took place as this book was in its final proofs in February 1994. This slaughter, like many similar atrocities in South Africa, indicates the danger of proposed peace deals, which attempt to restructure relationships of conflict without removing the underlying injustices. Such deals will not satisfy popular aspirations for freedom and national rights. Yet, by destabilising existing arrangements, they may well provoke a backlash from those who have a stake in the status quo. Though the long-running talks between the Palestine Liberation Organisation and the Israeli state may appear to have gained little for the Palestinians, even token recognition of Palestinian national rights is enough to inflame the fears of the Jewish settlers and their supporters. A political associate of the Hebron assassin explained that 'he wanted to stop the so-called peace process and save the state of Israel' (*Guardian*, 26 February 1994). The parallels with Northern Ireland, where zealous defenders of the existing order are also highly armed and vengeful are as clear as they are ominous.

It is an important time to ask questions and take stock. The situation is too fluid and the process at too early a stage to permit categorical answers. We need, however, to get our bearings, to get some purchase on the new dynamics that are at work. In Northern Ireland, there are many constants: partition, British troops, a disaffected nationalist minority and a loyal Unionist majority within the Northern state. There is also much that is new and which we need to understand if we are not to be overtaken by events.

In that spirit this book seeks to identify and explore the main factors which are giving shape and direction to the current conflict. We begin, in Chapter One, with the Downing Street declaration of December 1993. Whatever the immediate outcome of the declaration, it marks a significant shift in the approach of the British government towards the Union, in response to a perhaps more significant softening of the Irish republican commitment to national self-determination.

Despite the historic importance of relations between the world's first superpower and its oldest colony, the international dimension is unfortunately often neglected in contemporary studies of the Irish Troubles. In Chapter Two, we focus on the influence on Ireland of the New World Order inaugurated by the collapse of the Soviet Union and its global influence. Today, the Western powers enjoy a new authority in world affairs, nationalism has become a dirty word and anti-imperialist struggles appear to have become obsolete. The eclipse of mass popular involvement in nationalist movements everywhere has encouraged conservative trends and tendencies towards compromise, often on unfavourable terms. Whether acknowledged or not, these factors bear down heavily on the current phase of Anglo-Irish conflict.

The main impetus towards some form of negotiated settlement in Northern Ireland has come from the Irish republican movement, for the past two decades the leading force in the struggle for national liberation. In Chapter Three, we survey the evolution of Sinn Fein's peace policy as a response to the intense pressures of military occupation, Loyalist terror and political isolation. The peace process has brought to the fore a relatively unremarked but deep-rooted tendency in Irish republicanism towards compromise and constitutional politics.

It is understandable that, after more than 20 years of a bitter conflict that has left scarcely a single family untouched, the nationalist people in Northern Ireland should be weary and desperate for any sort of settlement. In these circumstances the republican leadership may consider that it has no alternative but to talk terms with Britain. Indeed there is no dishonour in negotiating a compromise with superior forces, not even in defeat. But it is crucial that any such setback is candidly acknowledged, not ignored or disguised or wished away.

The problems arise—and this is already clear in South Africa and Palestine—when unsatisfactory compromises enforced by imperial might are presented by nationalist politicians as advances towards justice and peace achieved through skilful diplomacy. The result of such cynical manoeuvres can only be confusion and demoralisation, compounding the effect of the already unfavourable balance of forces against the popular masses. Before it is possible to move forward, it is necessary to face the reality of past failures, to confront political weaknesses and learn from mistakes. It is in this spirit that we offer an appraisal of the politics of modern republicanism.

The dream of imposing terms on the Irish republican movement and posing as the agents of a dramatic settlement of the long-running Northern conflict inspires the governments in London and Dublin. Yet, though such an outcome might provide a temporary boost to two lacklustre premiers, they risk intensifying problems of legitimacy throughout Ireland and Britain with quite unpredictable consequences.

The deep confusions of the newly plural political culture of the South are the subject of Chapter Four. Here the parochial nationalism that gave the 26-county state its identity in the decades after partition is now submerged. Cultural identity is the new sectarianism, and fear of change is the dominant mood. Though Taoiseach (prime minister) Albert Reynolds won increased popularity with the launch of the Downing Street declaration, he faces an uncertain future.

Will there be a 'peace dividend' in the North? Chapter Five surveys the impact of the war on six-county society and points to the potentially destabilising effects of the end of the conflict. Not only has it now been going on for a generation, but much of the economic, social and political life of Northern Ireland has become reorganised around the war.

The exhaustion of politics in Britain and the crisis of legitimacy confronting its ruling elite have lent a new unpredictability to British policy in Ireland. Chapter Six examines the importance of the Union to the British state and the potential dangers of putting it in question.

It is on the complex conjunction of these factors that the future of Northern Ireland depends. Given their contradictory and unstable character, little is certain. It is, however, difficult to see an early end to military occupation, sectarian murder and the daily discrimination still suffered by the nationalist community in Northern Ireland. All this seems set to continue, and to continue to generate resistance in one form or another.

This book began life as a paper for a conference at the University of North London in February 1993 on the theme 'Has Ireland Come of Age?'. The conference was organised by the Irish Freedom Movement and supported by the University of North London Irish Studies Centre, the *Irish Post, Fortnight* magazine, and the University of East London Irish Society. It was a day of open, lively and informed debate among people of very different views. We could do with more discussion like that, and this book is designed to stimulate it. Events have moved on since then, and that paper has become this book.

Chapter Three on the republican movement relies heavily on the research and writing of Andy Clarkson. The rest owes much to Mick

Hume, Phil Murphy, Mick Kennedy and Fiona Foster, though the final responsibility is my own.

Mark Ryan
February 1994

1

The price of peace

On 15 December 1993, British prime minister John Major and Irish Taoiseach Albert Reynolds issued what was heralded as a historic Joint Declaration in Downing Street, London. Both leaders jointly 'acknowledged that the most urgent and important issue facing the people of Ireland, North and South, and the British and Irish governments together, is to remove the causes of conflict, to overcome the legacy of history and to heal the divisions which have resulted, recognising that the absence of a satisfactory and lasting settlement of relationships between the peoples of both islands has contributed to continuing tragedy and suffering' (*Times*, 16 December 1993).

After centuries of conflict and 24 years of open war, this was truly an ambitious agenda. To achieve it the two leaders indicated that they were ready to reconsider the constitutional structure of both existing states. They boldly proclaimed that their aim was 'to foster agreement and reconciliation, leading to a new political framework founded on consent and encompassing arrangements within Northern Ireland, for the whole island and between these islands'.

Major affirmed that the British government had 'no selfish strategic or economic interest in Northern Ireland' and accepted that it was 'for the people of the island of Ireland alone, by agreement between the two parts respectively, to exercise their right of self-determination on the basis of consent, freely and concurrently given, North and South, to bring about a united Ireland, if that is their wish'. In this way Major signalled a more flexible British approach towards the Union between Great Britain and Northern Ireland and acknowledged the legitimacy of Irish national aspirations.

1

In response, Reynolds indicated that the Dublin government was ready to renounce its constitutional claim to jurisdiction over the North.

The most important aspect of the declaration was tucked away in its concluding paragraphs. The two leaders asserted that 'the achievement of peace must involve a permanent end to the use of, or support for, paramilitary violence':

> They confirm that, in these circumstances, democratically mandated parties which establish a commitment to exclusively peaceful methods and which have shown that they abide by the democratic process, are free to participate fully in democratic politics and to join in dialogue in due course between the governments and the political parties on the way ahead.

At the heart of the Downing Street declaration lay the proposal that, were the Irish Republican Army to declare 'a cessation' of its long-running military campaign, leaders of its political wing, Sinn Fein, could—within three months, according to informal assurances—have a place at the conference table.

The Irish question transformed

The Major-Reynolds declaration marked an important advance in the Irish 'peace process'. While subsequent discussion focused on the response from the Irish republican movement, it was often forgotten that this process was launched by Sinn Fein with the adoption of the policy document 'Towards a lasting peace' at the Ard Fheis (national conference) in Dublin in February 1992. It continued through 1993 with talks between Sinn Fein president Gerry Adams and John Hume, leader of the moderate nationalist Social Democratic and Labour Party (SDLP), and with further talks between Hume and the Dublin government. As documents leaked at various stages from all sides revealed, extensive secret diplomacy continued alongside public exchanges, notably between Sinn Fein and the British government.

The initial response of the republican movement to the Downing Street declaration was one of disappointment at the failure of the

British government to state explicitly its approval of Irish unity, even as a distant aim. Despite the long-expressed desire of Sinn Fein leaders for a negotiated settlement, lack of enthusiasm for the Joint Declaration among Northern nationalists and republican activists dictated a policy of delay and equivocation. Given the persistence and intensity of the conflict, achieving a resolution would inevitably take time and involve a period of uncertainty and confusion.

After nearly a quarter of a century of war, leaving more than 3000 dead and many thousands more maimed and brutalised, there can be no mistaking the desire for peace. This is nowhere stronger than in the nationalist community in Northern Ireland, which has borne the brunt of military coercion and Loyalist terror, not to mention continuing sectarian discrimination and poverty. But does the 'peace process' offer a way towards peace? In the two years since the launch of Sinn Fein's peace policy there has been a dramatic upsurge in murderous Loyalist attacks, directed at republican activists as well as randomly at Catholics, and a higher profile for British Army repression, with more soldiers on the streets, stronger Border fortifications and more intrusive surveillance towers.

There is much to suggest that the continuation of the current process is likely to lead to more bloodshed and suffering for the Irish people. Though the Downing Street declaration may not go far enough in acknowledging the legitimacy of aspirations towards Irish unity to satisfy many republicans, it goes far enough to inflame Loyalist fears and animosities. Indeed, even the 1985 Anglo-Irish agreement, which brought the Dublin government into formal discussions about the North and signalled a decline in British enthusiasm for the Union, provoked an upsurge in Loyalist mobilisation and paramilitary violence. Whenever the republican movement talks about peace or offers to negotiate with the British government, the Loyalists, fearing a British retreat from the Union—the long-feared great betrayal—reach for their guns.

The trend towards more sectarian violence was already clear before the Downing Street declaration. In September 1993, the IRA observed a *de facto* one-week ceasefire in Belfast while an American delegation promoting the peace process was in town. In seven days, four Catholics were murdered by Loyalist gangs. The immediate response of the Loyalist paramilitary Ulster Freedom Fighters (UFF) to the announcement of talks between Adams and Hume was a declaration that violence against the nationalist community 'would intensify' (*Guardian*, 8 October 1993). It was no idle threat. Within three weeks 13 Catholics had been slaughtered by Loyalist gangs.

Whatever the immediate outcome of talks in the wake of the Downing Street declaration, the 'peace process' is set to continue. Its advance over the past two years reflects far-reaching changes in Ireland and in relations between Ireland and Britain. Before considering recent events further, it is first important to clarify the historic significance of Ireland in British politics and to indicate why the Irish Troubles have been the most serious threat to the British establishment since the Second World War.

One lesson of Irish history on which John Major might fruitfully reflect is that administrative solutions, though often successful temporary expedients, often store up problems for the future. The 1801 Act of Union was Britain's response to the rising of the United Irishmen in 1798. It aimed to contain colonial revolt in Ireland by integrating it into the British state: from the beginning of the nineteenth century Ireland was therefore no longer formally a colony, but part of the United Kingdom. The weakness of this constitutional device was that it incorporated within the borders of the kingdom a substantial body of Irish nationalists who continued to regard the Crown as the symbolic head of an occupying power. The fact that this mass of disaffected and disloyal citizens was not only included within the state, but represented in increasing numbers at Westminster, made Ireland a permanent source of instability in nineteenth-century Britain.

In 1921 another British government devised another ingenious solution to the Irish problem—partition. This scheme divided the country, the nationalist movement and the working class and allowed Britain to restore stability to Ireland after a decade of mounting strife. But the price of this solution was the inclusion within the Northern state of 500 000 nationalists under an even more coercive regime than the one that had prevailed throughout Ireland before partition. It was only a matter of time before the nationalists in the North began to demand their rights. But when they did, they immediately threatened the very integrity of the United Kingdom and therefore the authority of the British state itself.

The status of Northern Ireland as an integral part of the United Kingdom meant that the demand for Irish national rights implied the dismantling of the British state. The demand for national self-determination was threat enough when it came from third world colonies such as India, Malaya, Ghana or Kenya. But such states could be granted independence without putting the structure of the British state in jeopardy. Coming from Irish nationalists, the menace was of a different order. The threat to the state inherent in the demand for Irish freedom placed Irish republicanism outside the framework of domestic politics. Unlike every other political movement of modern times, republicanism did not consent to the rule of the British state. The withdrawal of consent inherent in Irish republicanism explains its explosive character in British politics. This is why the military activities of the IRA and other groups, even though relatively small in scale, are such a threat. They serve as a constant reminder to the British ruling class of the fragility of its position. In particular, the authorities fear that others who lack much of a stake in the system may come to identify with the withdrawal of consent to law and order characteristic of Irish republicans. The potential impact of the Irish War on class relations in Britain has long been an establishment preoccupation.

The determination of the British establishment to prevent any linkage between British workers and Irish republicans has dictated an intransigent line against nationalist demands in Northern Ireland from the start of the current Troubles. The ruling class cannot contemplate conceding Irish independence and allowing republicans to act as an example of a successful withdrawal of consent to other sections of the UK population. The instinctive unity of the mainstream parties on all substantial matters related to Ireland reflects their recognition of the peculiar danger of Irish republicanism.

The unique character of the Irish War has given it a central significance in British politics over the past two decades. The British establishment has successfully presented 'IRA terrorism' as a threat, not so much to itself, but to the entire British nation. The potential danger from Ireland has been turned into a focus for national unity and chauvinist prejudice, helping to foster a more conservative climate with much wider consequences.

At the same time, for those seeking to rally resistance against the conservative trends of British society in favour of a broader agenda for progress and change, the Irish liberation struggle was a key issue. Promoting identification with the Irish cause and organising solidarity with the republican movement were mandatory features in any serious anti-capitalist programme. The transformation of the Irish question and its place in British politics in the course of the current 'peace process' puts these underlying assumptions of past solidarity activity in question.

To grasp the dynamic at work in Anglo-Irish relations and the consequences for those hostile to British imperialism and sympathetic to the cause of Irish freedom, it is necessary to examine recent events in Ireland and Britain in a wider international context.

The national question in the New World Order

The fall of the Berlin Wall in November 1989 symbolised the demise of the Eastern bloc and the end of the historic division of Germany, Europe and the rest of the world between the rival camps of the Cold War. The process of disintegration continued in the Soviet Union itself, leading to economic breakdown and, by the end of 1991, the break-up of the Soviet state itself. The rapid, and unexpected, disappearance of the regime against which the West had maintained a constant level of political and military mobilisation for four decades sent shock waves around the world.

American president George Bush proclaimed the New World Order during the Gulf War in January 1991. The changing balance of forces since the end of the Cold War has dramatically strengthened the position of the Western powers, against the former Soviet Union and Eastern Europe and against third world countries and movements fighting for national liberation. Western governments now have a free hand to interfere directly in the affairs of other countries, staging elections (Cambodia), despatching troops (Somalia, Panama, Bosnia), or imposing settlements on long-standing conflicts (Namibia, South Africa, Israel/Palestine).

The most striking feature of the New World Order is that the Western powers assume the right to intervene in defiance of the national rights of other countries, usually offering humanitarian concern to legitimise their actions. At the same time, there is little sign of any mass resistance to Western intervention taking the form of support for nationalist movements. The collapse of the Soviet Union has discredited socialist, nationalist, even oppositional politics everywhere.

The distinctive feature of the current period is that the strategy of nationalist development appears singularly unattractive. The plight of Bosnia, a region that was forced to try to build a nation in response to the break-up of Yugoslavia, is not one likely to inspire emulation. In countries like Algeria and Vietnam, national liberation movements won historic victories over imperialist powers in the postwar period, but have since been reduced to pleading to be allowed back into the Western fold. The new-found modesty of these countries in their relations with the West provides a graphic illustration of the failure of the nationalist experiment.

For most of the twentieth century, the dream of national liberation has inspired mass resistance to the West—at the end of the First World War (in India, Egypt and Ireland), after the Second World War (in Asia and Africa), in the 1960s and 1970s (in South-East Asia, Latin America, southern Africa and Ireland). Today there is no mass enthusiasm for national independence and the quest for nationhood appears more as the response of one section of society to the disintegration of a wider political entity—as in the former Soviet Union and Eastern Europe.

The absence of popular pressure for national independence gives nationalist movements a narrower and more conservative character. National liberation movements with mass support among workers or peasants emphasised anti-capitalist as well as anti-imperialist goals. Hence the historic association between socialist and communist movements and national liberation struggles. The mass basis of national liberation movements tended to push them in a democratic, progressive, outward-looking direction. They attempted to transcend divisions imposed or fostered by the imperial authorities—divisions of class and caste, race, gender, ethnicity or religion. In general, the greater their success in overcoming such divisions, the greater their success in prosecuting the anti-imperialist struggle.

By contrast, the new wave of nationalists, who attract active support from only a section of the middle classes, tend towards a more elitist, reactionary and atavistic outlook. This trend is clearest in the nationalist movements that have emerged in the former Soviet Union and elsewhere in Eastern Europe, though it is also evident in Western Europe and beyond. Such groupings tend to be racist and anti-Semitic, demagogic and authoritarian. They enjoy reviving obscurantist religious rituals and dead languages, and have a penchant for historical commemorations. Their attachment to blood and soil, culture and tradition, gives them an exclusivist, backward-looking character.

The inherent conservatism of today's nationalist movements means that, though they are fiercely patriotic, they are reluctant to challenge the framework of Western domination which is the ultimate guarantor of their own interests. The demand for national independence from such movements is generally a claim from some elite group for recognition or resources rather than an attempt to defend or advance democratic rights. Hence they are inclined to restrict their nationalist fervour to the cultural sphere while adopting a conciliatory approach towards imperialist authority in the spheres of economics and politics. Indeed, from Sudan to Yugoslavia, the encouragement of local 'nationalisms' has become a mechanism for tighter Western domination. Such 'national struggles' have no anti-imperialist content.

Because of its peculiar relationship to Britain, Ireland often seemed remote from the patterns of Cold War politics in Europe, an appearance of being exceptional that has been reinforced by two decades of war. Yet, as we consider further in Chapter 2, Anglo-Irish relations have always been influenced by wider international considerations and they have been dramatically affected by the changes of the New World Order. Like oppositional movements everywhere, the Irish republican movement has been affected by the demise of the Soviet Union and the pervasive sense of the futility of attempts to change the world through mass struggle. For example, the sense of isolation of the republican movement must inevitably be reinforced by the difficulty in assembling a platform of representatives of radical nationalist movements from overseas, long a familiar feature of republican rallies. In Ireland, as in other countries, the climate of cynicism and low expectations has taken its toll on popular engagement in the nationalist cause.

The decline in popular nationalist sentiment everywhere in Ireland apart from the republican heartlands in the North, in particular throughout the South, has inevitably had a major impact on Irish republicanism. The absence of mass pressure on the republican leadership has led to a scaling down of objectives as the movement has assumed a more inward-looking character. Whereas in the past, republican platforms echoed to proclamations of the goal of victory and 'Brits out', in recent years demands have been scaled down to requests for a place at the negotiating table. As it has become confined to parts of the North over the past few years, the republican movement has retreated from its traditional aspiration to unite 'Catholic, Protestant and Dissenter' to assume the role of representative of a section of the Northern Catholic community. These trends have been encouraged by Sinn Fein's growing involvement in local government and community affairs in nationalist areas of the North.

However, before looking more closely at the impact of recent international events on the republican movement, we need to consider how they have influenced the British establishment and its approach towards Ireland.

Britain's changing Irish policy

Though the collapse of the Soviet Union boosted the morale and confidence of the Western powers, the ending of the Cold War was by no means an unalloyed triumph. It brought to a precipitate end the whole framework that had ensured stability in international relations and domestic politics for 40 years. These problems were immediately exacerbated by the descent of Western capitalism into another recessionary downturn, the third since the early 1970s. By the early 1990s, the capitalist world was in the grip of the deepest slump since the 1930s with little prospect of early recovery. The problems of political insecurity and economic stagnation were particularly acute in Britain whose chronic imperial decline had been forestalled through the postwar years through its 'special relationship' with the USA. As the USA itself could no longer sustain the hegemonic role that had been the key to postwar stability, Britain's future status as a world power seemed increasingly in doubt.

The paradox of enhanced global authority coexisting with the erosion of the basis of British imperial power was paralleled in the domestic sphere. The Conservative Party, traditional representative of the ruling class, despite presiding over a remorseless economic slump, again defeated the Labour Party in the 1992 election, inaugurating its fourth consecutive term in office. Yet, under the lacklustre leadership of John Major, the Tory Party was soon riven by factional strife, as leading Tories put personal ambitions and allegiances over party unity. The Conservatives were unable to give a clear expression to the interests of the British ruling class. The government staggered from one crisis to the next and one scandal to the next.

In former years, the Conservative Party was blessed with a clearly defined rogues' gallery of class enemies against which to define its own interests: the Soviet Union abroad, and the trade unions and the Labour Party at home. But now that has all gone and the British ruling class has lost cohesion. The tendencies to disintegration unleashed by the combination of the end of the Cold War and the continuing descent into slump were no longer contained by the old mechanisms of party loyalty or class solidarity. As a result, elements within the establishment no longer felt any restraint about calling into question traditional sources of authority and legitimacy. Even the monarchy, discredited by some of its junior members to the general amusement of the public, became the focus of open criticism, even condemnation, from the formerly deferential mass media.

The general loss of coherence of the British ruling class, which originated outside its relations with Ireland, nonetheless had important consequences for its Irish policy. In the past, the monolithic unity of the British establishment in the face of the Irish menace meant that there was no possibility of any new policy emerging outside the mainstream commitment to enforce the Union. Now both the monolith and the menace appeared to be crumbling, creating openings for the emergence of a new approach.

The characteristic feature of the New World Order is that it has made the unthinkable not only thinkable, but possible. If De Klerk could shake hands with Mandela, and Rabin with Arafat, why not Major with Adams? Such a policy always carries a high risk—it may exacerbate the instability which allowed it to emerge, intensifying the crisis of legitimacy of the ruling class. The visit of Gerry Adams to the USA in February 1994, where he was able to play the part of a visiting statesman, to the considerable embarrassment of the British government, indicated the dangers of the Downing Street declaration in bringing Sinn Fein into the mainstream. On the other hand, by providing a way of incorporating an erstwhile threat to the regime into a resolution on the terms of the authorities, it may consolidate their legitimacy, turning adversity to advantage.

Paradoxically, the British establishment's lack of cohesion in the climate created by the New World Order gives it greater flexibility in relation to Ireland. As British policy becomes less clearly defined, unorthodox initiatives stand a chance. In this situation the interests of different establishment factions may converge. One lobby with a clear interest in scaling down Britain's commitments in Ireland is the armed forces. At a time when the British military is feeling over-stretched in Nato and is under heavy pressure to reduce the financial burden of its operations, a reduction in the demands from Northern Ireland—where they have been increasing rather than decreasing in recent years—would be most welcome.

The location chosen to make the Joint Declaration—Downing Street—indicates another source of pressure for a change of Irish policy. After a series of public relations disasters the resident at No10 is desperate to demonstrate some achievement to the British public and the world. 'If he could pull that one off', declared one adviser, 'it would be our Falklands', recalling how Mrs Thatcher's foreign policy success transformed her position in the polls and paved the way for her victory in 1983 (*Economist*, 6 November 1993). When he became leader of the Conservative Party after the enforced departure of Margaret Thatcher in November 1990, nobody would have given high odds on Major's chances of pulling off a settlement of the Irish War. Yet, three years later, the shifting views of the leadership of the republican movement gave him considerable grounds for optimism.

From national liberation to inclusive dialogue

The background to the shift of the republican movement from an emphasis on the armed struggle to proposals for a negotiated settlement was eloquently summarised by leading Sinn Fein member Jim Gibney, a prominent advocate of the 'peace process', in his keynote address at the annual Wolfe Tone commemoration at Bodenstown in County Kildare in June 1992:

> For republicans, these have been difficult years. We have spent them in a penurious state and have visited much hardship on our families; we have spent long terms behind bars; we have shouldered the bodies of many comrades to their resting place; we have spent hours on end at meetings and tramped the countryside to hold in place the sinews of struggle. We are constantly surrounded with the human consequences of a bloody and protracted conflict....
>
> Against such an intense, self-sacrificing background, it is important on this Bodenstown Sunday that we ask ourselves, out loud, does this reality mean that republicans have been deafened by the "deadly sound of our own gunfire"? Does this reality mean that republicans are trapped inside a complex web of struggle from which they can't or won't emerge, hostages to an immediate past because of all the pain, suffering and commitment to past views, expressed trenchantly, which in time solidified into unyielding principles?
>
> Does this reality mean that republicans are incapable of recognising that there is a different world to the one that existed in the mid-sixties or that they ignore the more recent changes sweeping across the globe? (*An Phoblacht/Republican News*, 25 June 1992)

Lest there be any doubt about the consequences of his speech, Gibney spelled them out in the following week's *An Phoblacht/ Republican News*: 'The conflict has gone on long enough. It is now time to engage in talks to find a peaceful way towards a new Ireland.' (25 June 1992)

Gibney's elevation of the diplomatic 'peace process' launched at the Ard Fheis four months earlier over the armed struggle did not go down well with some activists at Bodenstown. No doubt many republicans were sceptical that talks could bring about the peace for which they had given so much. At the same time, there was a growing sentiment that there was little further to be gained by carrying on the struggle in its current form. In the absence of any alternative strategy emerging from any section of the movement to challenge the leadership line, this sentiment became stronger over the next 18 months, and the peace process acquired an air of inevitability.

Gibney candidly acknowledged the war-weariness of the nationalist community and the sense that the movement had reached an impasse. He presented the 'peace process' as a response to this recognition and to the new international situation. It was at Bodenstown 15 years earlier that Jimmy Drumm had announced the new emphasis of the republican movement on the political sphere as a means of breaking the military deadlock and overcoming the movement's isolation. It was more than 10 years since the hunger-strikes and Sinn Fein's subsequent election successes had confirmed the extent of support for the nationalist struggle in the North. Yet in the following decade Sinn Fein had signally failed to break out of its heartlands in the North to overcome the influence of the moderate nationalist Social Democratic and Labour Party; much worse, at election after election, it had failed to break through in the South. Gibney's recognition of the impasse faced by the republican movement was unavoidable.

Faced with the overwhelming might of the British state, the IRA has shown resilience and determination. Despite repeated British assertions over the years that it was on the verge of military defeat, the IRA had confirmed that it could not be beaten. Yet, though the IRA could survive, the republican leadership had long acknowledged that it could not on its own drive the British out. The result was a prolonged stalemate, but one, as Gibney indicated, that was sustained at the cost of enormous sacrifice and suffering by the movement itself. In the early 1990s, after more than 20 years of war, the nationalist community faced *increasing* levels of military harassment and an *increasing* incidence of Loyalist paramilitary attacks and assassinations. Without any prospect of achieving the goals of Irish unity or independence, the suffering of the nationalist community was becoming unbearable.

Furthermore, the emphasis put by the republican movement on the electoral sphere inevitably created tensions with the IRA's continuing military campaign. Anti-republican propaganda focusing on particular IRA shootings and bombings helped to prevent Sinn Fein winning wider support North and South. The more that the Sinn Fein leadership pursued the 'peace process', the more the military campaign came to be seen as a part of the problem instead of being a part of the solution.

The combined effect of the pressures on the republican movement from international and domestic sources was to produce a lowering of horizons and a narrowing of outlook. The clearest indication of the new pragmatism of the republican leadership came with the talks in 1993 between Sinn Fein's Gerry Adams and the leader of the SDLP, John Hume. Though the talks proceeded in confidence, the republican movement's willingness to fudge the issue of national self-determination was clear in its public statements that year.

'We would like to see a 32-county republic in Ireland', said Derry Sinn Fein leader Martin McGuinness, 'but what we're trying to bring about is a situation where all the people of Ireland get a right to national self-determination' (*Guardian,* 18/19 September 1993). Adams expanded on this cryptic formulation: 'Whatever agreement we come up with has to be an agreement that the Unionists, like the rest of us, can give their allegiance to. They have to be part of it and have to feel that it accommodates them.' (*Independent on Sunday,* 3 October 1993) In a speech at Cookstown on the twenty-fifth anniversary of the launch of the civil rights movement, McGuinness returned to the theme of 'national reconciliation' between the Unionists and the rest of the Irish people. 'Any new agreement', he insisted, 'must respect the diversity of our different traditions and must earn their allegiance and agreement' (*AP/RN,* 30 September 1993).

The tortuous formulations of the republican movement's goals in 1993 contrast sharply with Gerry Adams' clear statement of the importance of national rights in 1988, in the wake of a previous round of talks with John Hume:

When a people are divided in political allegiance, the democratic principle is that majority rights should prevail; the more so when such fundamentals as national rights are in question....

The exercise of the right to national self-determination in practice involves, primarily, the acceptance of Irish national rights by the British government. ('SDLP "confused" on self-determination —SF', *Irish Times*, 13 September 1988)

It appeared that over the intervening five years the confusions of the SDLP had been assimilated by Sinn Fein.

Adams' 1988 response to the SDLP leader states with exemplary clarity the basic issue of the Irish conflict: the denial of the national rights of the Irish people by Britain. There can be no flexibility on such a fundamental issue: Ireland can either be independent or ruled by Britain. Concessions to Unionist 'difference' mean in practice abandoning the national rights of the majority. It is important to point out that the Loyalists neither have nor claim any 'national' rights. Their 'loyalty' is to Britain and to its suppression of the national rights of the majority of the Irish people. When republicans declare their respect for the political allegiances of the Unionists, they effectively give up their own struggle for national liberation.

In the 1970s, republicans emphasised the goal of 'victory' and any negotiations were conducted around publicised lists of preconditions regarding prisoners, troops, time periods, etc. In the 1980s, the demand was for 'British withdrawal' within a specified period. In Sinn Fein's 1992 document the earlier terms disappeared, to be replaced with appeals for a 'democratic resolution' of the conflict, for 'talks without preconditions' and for an 'inclusive dialogue' among all concerned parties.

Adams explained to delegates at the February 1992 Ard Fheis that 'in effect, the document ['Towards a lasting peace'] calls upon London and Dublin to initiate a process of national reconciliation in Ireland' (*AP/RN*, 27 February 1992). That the republican movement should look to the seats of government of the occupying power and its stooges in Ireland—the very forces responsible for maintaining national division—to advance the project of 'national reconciliation' indicates that, in effect, the movement has abandoned the goal of national liberation.

The narrowing of outlook of the Irish republican movement is evident in its steady drift away from radicalism towards more moderate postures. Over the past decade it has dropped its strident condemnations of the 'Stoop Down Low Party' and its middle class character, in favour of promoting 'pan-nationalist' unity, particularly in local government and community matters. Sinn Fein leaders have adopted a notably deferential attitude to mainstream politicians and towards the churches, particularly the Catholic church, which continues to exert a malign influence over Irish society, North and South. In its quest for respectability, Sinn Fein leaders can be found endorsing all the conventional moral panics over issues such as drugs, Aids and child sexual abuse, despite the role of such campaigns in strengthening authoritarian trends in society.

When, in June 1993, Irish president Mary Robinson shook hands with Adams during a visit to Belfast there was some protest that she was conferring respectability on terrorism. But, as Derry journalist Eamonn McCann pointed out, the more significant question was 'what's up with the Provos that they're now shaking hands with Free State presidents?' (E McCann, *War and an Irish Town*, 1993, p36). He recalled that in the past when leading representatives of the Dublin government had come North they had been met with pickets protesting about extradition, repression and censorship: 'now the request is that Sinn Fein leaders should be allowed to pay their respects.'

The Robinson handshake symbolised another aspect of the narrowing of the republican outlook. Adams justified his right to meet Robinson on the grounds that republicans were 'a substantial and active part' of the nationalist community of West Belfast (*AP/RN*, 24 June 1993). In the past, the republican movement aspired to unite the Irish people in the cause of national freedom from British domination. Now its leaders humbly seek recognition as representatives of particular local communities. In response to the pressures of isolation, the republican movement has retreated into its own heartlands, emphasising the distinctive culture and traditions that reinforce its distance from other sections of Irish society. The result is that republicanism risks approximating its caricature as a conservative and Catholic movement.

The new balance of forces between Britain and the Irish republican movement has made possible much that was previously unthinkable. It is still the case that the British state cannot militarily defeat the IRA without imposing a level of coercion that would risk serious disturbances in both Ireland and Britain. Yet military victory may be rendered unnecessary by political success in exploiting the weakness of the republican movement. In this sense the 'peace process' is the new form through which the London and Dublin governments are pursuing their war against the IRA. It will not be successful overnight, but it has already helped to create a climate in which, even if sections of the republican movement were to carry on the armed struggle, the national struggle is unlikely to assume the same significance in Anglo-Irish relations that it did in the past.

For those committed to promoting an anti-imperialist and internationalist response to British domination over Ireland, the emphasis must shift from upholding national rights to a more direct challenge to imperialist intervention. Whatever else may change, two things remain certain. Britain can never play a progressive role in Ireland and a British withdrawal remains the precondition for peace.

2

Ireland in the New World Order

6 September 1993: Oral message from the British government

Sinn Fein should comment in as major a way as possible on the PLO/Rabin deal; that Sinn Fein should be saying "If they can come to an agreement in Israel, why not here? We are standing at the altar why won't you come and join us". ('Setting the record straight'— Sinn Fein's record of the communications between Sinn Fein and the British government, October 1990—November 1993, p41)

Whatever the outcome of the PLO/Israel deal, the message which emerges, as it has elsewhere, is that discussion and inclusiveness are the way forward in all conflicts. It is a lesson for the learning, not only for the British, but also for the Dublin government. (*An Phoblacht/Republican News*, 16 September 1993)

In the wake of the historic handshake between Israeli prime minister Yitzhak Rabin and Yasser Arafat, head of the Palestine Liberation Organisation, on 13 September 1993, many asked—why not in Ireland too? All over the world former enemies, some with records of bloody conflict going back further than the present phase of the Troubles in Ireland, were apparently laying down arms and sitting around conference tables. If this could be done in the Middle East, in South-East Asia, even in South Africa, then surely it could happen in Northern Ireland.

The recognition that international factors have some bearing on events in Ireland is a welcome change from the insular way in which the

Irish War has often been perceived. Over the past 25 years, the conflict in Northern Ireland has often been considered in isolation from global influences. Indeed, even Britain itself, the key player in the conflict, has in many accounts been removed from the picture. The Irish War has been presented as an exception and as an enigma, a conflict rooted in the peculiarities of Irish history and the Irish psyche. Having little in common with other conflicts and few points of contact with outside influences, the Irish War has been depicted as difficult, if not impossible, for the outsider to understand and certainly impervious to political resolution.

Unfortunately, many attempts to look at developments in Ireland in the context of the rapid changes that have taken place internationally since the collapse of the Soviet Union have not only preserved the old prejudices, but have reinforced them. Britain's long-standing justification for its role in Northern Ireland—its humanitarian commitment to end sectarian strife and reconcile warring communities—has received retrospective endorsement from the growing scale of British interference overseas since the late 1980s, in the Gulf, in the Kurdish crisis, in the former Yugoslavia (see M Freeman, *The Empire Strikes Back: Why We Need a New Anti-War Movement*, 1993). As a result, the real issues at stake in relations between Ireland and Britain are further obscured and mystified.

In this chapter we examine the international context of recent events in Ireland. To throw light on the current dynamic towards a settlement it is useful to contrast the years from 1968 to 1973 with the period from 1988 to the present. The conflict in Ireland erupted at a time when Western imperialism was on the defensive in the face of national liberation struggles around the world and their radical supporters in the West. Over the past few years, the Western powers have come to enjoy unprecedented confidence about intervening in the third world. Nationalist movements are everywhere in retreat together with oppositional forces in the West. But first, let's look at the broader historical significance of Anglo-Irish relations.

Britain's oldest colony

Our starting point is the recognition of the historic importance of the conflict between the world's first superpower and its oldest, nearest and most troublesome colony. Long before Britain consolidated its global empire in the years between 1880 and the First World War, it had subdued and integrated Ireland through a series of bloody wars over the previous two centuries. Long before the British ruling class had to confront colonial revolts in Asia and Africa, it gained vital experience in Ireland. This enabled Britain's imperial administrators to develop a range of strategies and tactics for dealing with insurgents that has stood them in good stead up to this day—and has given them an important advantage over their Western rivals.

As Britain's oldest colony, Ireland is home to the world's longest-established national liberation movement, one which has always had important relationships with liberation movements elsewhere. Theobald Wolfe Tone, the founder of Irish republicanism and the leader of the ill-fated 1798 rebellion, had close links with the revolutionary movements that flourished throughout Europe after the French Revolution. The Easter Rising in 1916 was celebrated by Lenin and the Bolsheviks as a blow to the heart of one of Europe's greatest empires at the height of the First World War and only 18 months before the Russian Revolution.

In the aftermath of the First World War there was a dramatic upsurge of nationalist movements seeking to take advantage of the collapse of old empires and the overstretch of those that emerged on the winning side. Many looked to the Irish republican movement as a guide and inspiration. To the relatively newly established nationalist organisations in India, Egypt and South Africa, Irish republicans had a long experience of different forms of struggle, from physical force through mass campaigning to parliamentary manoeuvring. When Ho Chi Minh, future leader of the Vietnamese struggle against the USA, was working as a dishwasher in a London hotel in 1920, he wept bitterly when he heard of the death on hunger-strike of Terence MacSwiney, Lord Mayor of Cork and fervent republican. Marcus Garvey, the Jamaican-born black nationalist founder of the 'Back to Africa' movement that won a worldwide following in the early 1920s, was a great admirer of the Irish nationalist leader Eamon de Valera.

Though the imperial strategy of 'divide and rule' pioneered by the Romans has become something of a cliche, in the modern era it has only been successfully deployed by Britain—and Britain polished its technique over the centuries in Ireland. While attempts by France, Germany, Italy, even the USA, have failed, forcing them to rely heavily on force, Britain has generally succeeded in avoiding coercion through the skilful use of political manoeuvres. Though violence is usually required in some degree, and is always in reserve, the favoured technique is to foster a political relationship with a section of colonial society, or even with a section of the nationalist movement, and to exploit these links to promote divisions within the indigenous population.

In Ireland, Britain has maintained close relations with the Protestants of Ulster ever since the authorities sponsored their settlement in the seventeenth century. In the nineteenth century, Britain faced recurring nationalist revolts in Ireland. Because Ireland had been fully incorporated into Britain in the 1801 Act of Union, these also caused disruption at home. In response it developed the technique of drawing the moderate leadership of the Irish nationalist movement into the mainstream of British parliamentary politics. Though the Irish Parliamentary Party led by Charles Stewart Parnell in the 1880s was a constant irritant to the government, it was to a considerable extent domesticated, and its policies moderated, through its association with the Liberal Party. In turn, the 'constitutional' nationalist politicians provided some restraint on the 'physical force' republicans active in the Irish countryside and in Britain.

In the years around the First World War, the containment of the threat from Irish nationalism was for the British establishment the test of its international authority, both within the Empire and further afield. After the war, Unionist leader Edward Carson warned the British government of the consequences of defeat in Ireland:

If you tell your empire in India, in Egypt, and all over the world that you have not got the men, the money, the pluck, the inclination and the backing to restore order in a country within 20 miles of your own shore, you may as well begin to abandon the attempt to make British rule prevail throughout the Empire at all. (Quoted in M Beloff, *Imperial Sunset,* Vol1, 1969, p315)

In response to the Irish demand for independence, British prime minister David Lloyd George observed:

> Suppose we gave it to them? It will lower the prestige and dignity of this country and reduce British authority to a low point in Ireland itself. It will give the impression that we have lost grip, that the Empire has no further force and will have an effect on India and throughout Europe. (Quoted in T Jones, *Whitehall Diary*, Vol3, 1971, p109)

Britain's determination to meet the challenge from Ireland led to partition—a settlement that became a colonial model.

Partition was the ideal colonial solution because it succeeded in dividing a nationalist movement that commanded majority support in Ireland. This allowed the British to step back and, in the course of the Civil War that followed in the South, let the section of the nationalist movement that they had cultivated slaughter the intransigent republicans. In the North, the British could rely on their long-established allies—the Loyalists—to enforce acquiescence to the new terms, which, with vicious pogroms, they duly did. Confronted with intractable colonial problems in the future—in Palestine, India, Cyprus—partition was to prove the great British solution. The debates that raged during the early 1990s over various ways of redrawing the map of Bosnia indicate the continuing appeal of this approach. Indeed there are even some Loyalists today who suggest that the 're-partition' of Northern Ireland into cantons might be the final solution to its problems.

The British authorities learned the value of always trying to distinguish between 'moderates' and 'extremists'. They subsequently sought to avoid alienating a nationalist movement in its entirety. When matters came to a head, the final resolution followed the pattern of the Irish Civil War and the 'moderates' were provided with whatever support they needed to wipe out the 'extremists' and so proceed to consolidate British rule by proxy. In Kenya, for example, the British cultivated the group around Jomo Kenyatta, who played a leading role in the Mau Mau revolt. Once the counter-insurgency operation against the more militant wing of the movement had been completed—at a cost of

50 000 lives—the way was clear for Kenyatta to emerge as head of state in an 'independent' Kenya.

Britain's success in colonial management played a key role in delaying its imperial decline, particularly in the years after the Second World War. In this period, France suffered humiliating and domestically destabilising defeats in Vietnam in 1954 and in Algeria in 1962; the USA had a similar experience in Vietnam in 1973. Despite considerable embarrassments in India, Malaya, Kenya, Cyprus, Aden and Suez, the British establishment managed to present decolonisation as an essentially benign and civilising process. This corresponded with the 'caring' image of the welfare state and allowed the British ruling class to act in an advisory capacity to its allies.

The dramatic success of partition ensured that no challenge from Ireland upset Britain through this critical period. The upsurge in national liberation struggles worldwide after the Second World War found little resonance in Ireland. While anti-colonialist movements flourished on every continent, Ireland remained quiescent. The IRA's attempt to revive the national struggle—in the Border campaign from 1956 to 1962—was a flop.

From civil rights to national liberation

The current phase of Anglo-Irish conflict began with the civil rights campaign in Northern Ireland in the late sixties. This challenge to the denial of democratic rights that is inherent in the framework of the six-county state provoked a repressive response from the local paramilitary police and Loyalists. After a police attack on a civil rights demonstration in Derry in October 1968, the movement rapidly gathered momentum—and so did the backlash. In response to intense rioting in Belfast and Derry in August 1969 British troops invaded, ostensibly to keep the peace, but in fact to enforce imperial authority. Continuing repression provoked the revival of the republican movement and the emergence of armed resistance.

When the British interned several hundred republican suspects in August 1971, mostly the wrong people, the conflict escalated rapidly. On Bloody Sunday, in January 1972, British paratroopers fired on a civil rights march in Derry, killing 14 people. On Bloody Friday in

July 1972 the IRA detonated 26 bombs in Belfast city centre, killing two soldiers and nine civilians. In the 12 months up to the end of 1972, 467 people were killed in Northern Ireland, more than in any year before or since.

The critical, and ultimately triumphant, phase of the Vietnam War took place at the same time as the upsurge in Ireland. In January 1968 the combined forces of North Vietnam and the insurgents in the South launched the Tet Offensive, a major onslaught in the heart of the occupied territories. Though the costs were high, and it did not achieve its immediate military objectives, it was a blow to the morale of the US forces and their puppet regime in Saigon from which they never recovered. By 1971, the USA was withdrawing—though also stepping up its lethal bombing raids. In 1972 the North Vietnamese army invaded, leading to intensive fighting, with heavy casualties all around. In January 1973 the USA announced a ceasefire and finally withdrew its forces, leaving all its local allies in the lurch.

Three factors in the international situation at this time contributed to the dramatic advance of liberation struggles. First, the imperialist powers were in a position of unprecedented weakness. Second, they faced national liberation movements at the height of their strength and international prestige. Third, the Western powers were constrained by the influence of mass protest and international solidarity movements at home. Let's take each in turn.

Imperialism on the defensive

By the late sixties, the morale of the imperialist powers was at an all-time low. From being a source of inspiration and pride at the turn of the century, imperialism had become widely associated with genocide, racism, plunder and war, and a source of embarrassment and shame to the West. In May 1900, the relief of the Boer siege of the British garrison at Mafeking in South Africa had prompted days of popular celebration in London and other British cities. More than 60 years later Western capitals were shaken by mass demonstrations in support of anti-imperialist struggles in South-East Asia, Africa and Latin America. What went wrong for the West?

Imperialism received its first blow with the First World War, when the link between imperialism and the drive to war became evident to millions in the course of the carnage in Europe. The postwar upsurge of anti-colonial revolts in Asia and the Middle East further undermined the moral authority of the West. Despite this setback, however, the ideology of imperialism remained in the ascendant through the inter-war years. The balance of public opinion in the West swung decisively against imperialism only after the Second World War. The impact of the world slump of the 1930s, the rise of fascism in Germany and else-where and the experience of the war itself threw imperialist ideology into disarray.

The exposure of the horrific consequences of imperialist notions of racial superiority in the Nazi Holocaust provoked a wave of revulsion against racism. Until then race had been a key justification for the West's mission to dominate the rest of the world. In the new sensibili-ties of the postwar period, racial policy was not just an embarrass-ment in the here and now, but a stain on what had been regarded as meritorious—the past record of colonial conquest. As all the Western powers were discredited by the exposure of the barbarous consequences of imperialism, national pride in the glories of Empire was replaced by a sense of guilt and shame.

The postwar retreat from Empire and the process of decolonisation further weakened imperialist morale. Despite Britain's skill in manag-ing imperial decline, tales of atrocities filtered back—from Malaya, from Kenya, from Aden—tarnishing cherished colonial myths and eroding imperial confidence. The Suez crisis in 1956 forced both Britain and France to come to terms with Arab nationalism and the ascendancy of the USA in the Middle East. By the mid-sixties, Britain's remaining global commitments were becoming a severe financial strain, contributing to the sterling crisis of 1967 and the decision to withdraw from 'east of Suez'.

The relative success of decolonisation was reflected in the fact that 1967 was the first year since the Second World War that Britain was not at war somewhere in the world. At the time, few noticed signs of the re-emergence of trouble in Ireland, which was shortly to revive bitter memories of the imperial past and put Britain on the defensive at home and abroad. An important influence on the new challenge from Ireland was the apparent success of liberation struggles around the world.

While the imperialist powers were on the defensive in the late sixties, the forces of national liberation were reaching the peak of their power. The Second World War gave a major boost to nationalist movements which had been growing in strength and militancy over the previous two decades. The consequences were most immediately apparent in Asia, where imperialist rule was weakest and most divided. The victory of the Chinese Revolution under Mao Zedong in 1949 was the most traumatic event for the Western world since the Russian Revolution in 1917. Not only did it remove a vast area and population from Western control, it provided an inspiration for liberation struggles around the world. For much of the next 30 years, radical nationalist movements in South-East Asia, in the Middle East and North Africa, in Latin America—particularly after the success of Fidel Castro in Cuba in 1959—and in southern Africa, remained the major threat to the authority of the Western ruling class.

Another important consequence of the Second World War was the emergence of the Soviet Union as a major world power. While the Western capitalist order had been discredited by the slump, fascism and war, Stalin's Soviet Union had acquired growing international prestige. When the Western rapprochement with Stalin broke down with the onset of the Cold War in 1947, the Soviet Union assumed the role of an alternative pole to Western capitalism. In particular, it provided third world nationalist movements with an alternative focus of allegiance and an alternative model of development. The existence of the Soviet model, reinforced after 1949 by China, gave a coherence and sense of destiny to national liberation movements, which they had often previously lacked. The adoption of radical political programmes enabled movements led by the middle classes to mobilise mass popular support in the struggle against imperialism.

The strength of Catholicism in Ireland made it highly susceptible to the anti-communist ideology of the Cold War. Though Ireland's feeble official communist movement came to exert growing influence on the residual elements of republicanism in the sixties, both remained marginal to Irish society. Ireland as a whole was secure against the radicalising influence of Stalinist third world nationalism. Yet the generally destabilising effect of the struggles of the third world did contribute to the unfolding of events in Ireland. At first this influence was mediated through the corrosive impact of third world liberation struggles in the Western powers themselves.

The rise of national liberation movements in the third world gave a stimulus to radical forces in the West. On the defensive for most of the postwar period because of the success of anti-communism, the left found inspiration in the often victorious struggles of the colonial world. From the early fifties, the left had been looking for a 'third way' between the rival Western and Eastern blocs; in the sixties it found it in the 'third world'—a term coined by the influential British periodical *New Left Review*. Solidarity with third world national liberation struggles became an organising principle of the Western left. In the late sixties, the movement in sympathy with the Vietnamese struggle against the USA became the focus of mass demonstrations and disruptions across the Western world. In the USA, the scale of these protests, reflecting divided counsels in the ruling elite itself, contributed to the domestic crisis that culminated in US withdrawal from Vietnam and the collapse of the Nixon presidency.

The rise of third world nationalism coincided with and reinforced a number of internal challenges to Western authority. In the USA, the demand for black civil rights had been gathering momentum since the early sixties. It reached a climax in the widespread rioting that followed the assassination of civil rights leader Martin Luther King in Memphis in April 1968. The following month in France a combination of student protests and a general strike precipitated a governmental crisis. Student revolt and industrial militancy swept the West over the next few years; the cause of women's liberation too became a focus of organisation, agitation and controversy.

When Ireland returned to international attention in the late sixties after decades of quiescence, one of the first figures to seize the limelight was Bernadette Devlin, a woman, a student and, in 1968 when she became involved in the civil rights movement, barely 20-years old. In March 1969 she was elected MP for mid-Ulster and, later in the year, she was sentenced to six months' imprisonment for 'incitement to riot' during the Battle of the Bogside in Derry in August 1969. Devlin subsequently recalled one of the first civil rights protests in August the previous year that had been blocked by the police from proceeding to its destination in Dungannon. In the style of the black civil rights protests in the USA, familiar from television reports, the marchers sat down in the road. One of the organisers, a veteran Stalinist trade union official, proposed that they sing 'the civil rights anthem—"We Shall Overcome"'. But, as yet, nobody knew the words. (B Devlin, *The Price of My Soul*, 1969, p93)

Though the student civil rights marchers soon learned the words of 'We Shall Overcome', many of the young nationalists rapidly drawn into the riots that inevitably followed civil rights protests were more comfortable singing traditional Irish rebel songs. And though the older generation of republicans who were influenced by the official communist movement favoured adopting radical third world terms such as 'national liberation front', they were soon swept aside by the forces of the emerging Provisional IRA who asserted their commitment to fighting the British forces in the terms of traditional republicanism.

Given the nature of the Northern state, the demand for equal rights for Catholics inevitably questioned its very existence, provoking a spiral of repression and resistance that culminated in war. Britain's inability to meet the demand for civil rights meant that it rapidly faced the demand for national liberation.

Bloody Sunday in Derry in January 1972 crystallised national and international trends in the evolution of the Anglo-Irish conflict. More than three years after the first civil rights protest in Derry—supported by only a few hundred people—had been baton-charged off the streets by the police, 30 000 people marched to demand the same rights in a city now under military occupation. The British response may have been a calculated gesture of intimidation after months of increasing republican resistance. Yet the fact that Britain resorted to such brutal tactics, so close to home and in view of the world's media, indicated a drastic failure in its more subtle colonial management strategies. The savagery of Bloody Sunday exposed Britain to condemnation around the world, reinforcing sentiments of imperial shame already running high over Vietnam, and putting Britain now, as well as the USA, in the dock.

Bloody Sunday was the most powerful catalyst for the transition between the civil rights movement and the Provisional IRA. It conferred legitimacy on the nationalist movement as the only force that could defend the Catholic community and on national liberation as the only future for Catholics in Northern Ireland. When the British embassy in Dublin was burned to the ground at the end of an angry demonstration in solidarity with the people of the North a week after Bloody Sunday, the potential for the conflict in the North to destabilise the whole of Ireland and undo the partition solution struck fear into the heart of the British establishment.

Furthermore, Bloody Sunday in Derry was followed by a protest march 30 000-strong in London. This attracted widespread support from the left and from young people radicalised around Vietnam and other third world issues, as well as from Irish people living in England. It culminated in a major riot in Whitehall when marchers insisted on delivering coffins symbolising each of the Derry dead to Downing Street. For a Western ruling class bracing itself for the impact of a humiliating defeat in Vietnam, events in Ireland had taken a menacing turn. The British state was on the defensive, the republican movement was in the ascendant and anti-imperialist solidarity in Britain was at its peak.

The moral rearmament of imperialism

The contrast between the balance of forces in Anglo-Irish relations in 1972 and that prevailing 20 years later could not be more striking. By the late eighties Britain had regained the initiative in Ireland. The IRA's armed struggle had reached a stalemate: it could survive, but it could not drive the British out. Meanwhile Sinn Fein's attempt to overcome the military stalemate in the political sphere had also reached an impasse: it had demonstrated its solid base in the North, but had failed to advance against the SDLP or, most importantly, to break through in the South. Meanwhile the British had stepped up the political pressure through the 1985 Anglo-Irish agreement and the military pressure through shoot-to-kill operations against republicans and Loyalist paramilitary attacks on Catholics in general.

Two decades after the National Liberation Front in Vietnam succeeded in ousting the Americans, the Irish republican movement is still fighting to oust the British. We examine elsewhere the internal factors which have contributed to the current state of affairs. Here we look more closely at the international factors, dramatically reversed since

1968. By the early nineties, the West was once again in the ascendant, third world nationalism was everywhere in retreat and popular protest movements of all kinds in disarray. Now all these forces were combining to push the Irish republican movement into negotiating a settlement with Britain.

At the close of the 1980s, a remarkable transformation occurred in the status of imperialism in the West. For decades the Western powers had enforced their will in the third world by stealth or disguised their interference as part of an anti-communist crusade. Now they went openly on the offensive against any threat to their interests in the third world, proclaiming their objectives to all and enforcing them militarily without remorse or restraint.

The key factor in the changing policy of the West towards the third world was the collapse of the Soviet Union as a superpower, leading to the precipitate end of 40 years of Cold War. Though the Soviet Union had never been a serious economic or political rival to the West, its success in developing a substantial military-industrial sector had allowed it to maintain the image of a superpower. The weakness of the capitalist system in the third world together with the rivalries among the imperialist powers had given the Soviet Union considerable room to manoeuvre throughout the postwar period. By the mid-eighties, however, the problems of stagnation and decline could no longer be disguised. Mikhail Gorbachev's reforms only accelerated economic disintegration and provoked a crisis of legitimacy for the Stalinist bureaucracy. The process of collapse began in Eastern Europe in 1989 and then extended into the Soviet Union itself, leading by 1991 to the fall of Gorbachev and the break-up of the Soviet state.

The first indication of the global significance of the end of the Cold War came in the Gulf War in February 1991. In response to the Iraqi annexation of Kuwait the preceding September, a US-led Western task force based in Saudi Arabia launched an onslaught of unprecedented ferocity on Iraq, resulting in an immediate death toll estimated at between 100 000 and 120 000 Iraqis—and 147 Western casualties. The Iraqi death toll within three months of the war's end was estimated at between 144 000 and 181 000 (*British Medical Journal*, 3 August 1991).

The Gulf War revealed not only the military superiority of the West, but also how far the moral rearmament of imperialism had proceeded. The conflict exposed a public opinion in the West largely purged of the sentiments of guilt and shame about imperialism that were characteristic of the postwar years. In their conduct of the war, the Western ruling classes proceeded with a new level of confidence and conviction. At least in the short term, the promotion of a third world bogeyman—Iraq's Saddam Hussein—as a replacement for the late Soviet Union guaranteed the cohesion of the Western alliance.

The Western victory in the Gulf War, after decades of strategic withdrawals if not outright defeats in the third world, boosted morale in all members of the alliance. The much smaller scale victory of Margaret Thatcher's government over Argentina in the Falklands War in 1982 had given her renewed confidence to take on the miners and other 'enemies within'. Now the more spectacular triumph over Iraq gave her successor an inkling that even he could deal with old enemies closer to home.

National liberation in retreat

The Gulf War also revealed how far the collapse of the Soviet Union had demoralised third world resistance. While the end of the Cold War came suddenly in the West, in the third world it was more the culmination of a long process of disillusionment. In the 1970s, despite the anti-colonial rhetoric of the Brezhnev era, the Soviet Union played little part in the wave of revolts in South-East Asia, southern Africa and central America that followed the US defeat in Vietnam. Radical nationalist movements were often forced to fight alone against the superior forces of the Western powers. The result was the devastation of economic life in many of these countries, creating insuperable problems for the new regimes. In other cases, such as Nicaragua and Iran, the Soviet Union backed the corrupt old dictators to the bitter end. Yet, given the weak position of the Western powers, the Soviet Union's foreign policy enabled it to preserve its reputation as a patron of third world nationalism.

By the late eighties, however, the demise of Soviet influence in the third world was apparent. Two factors were decisive: growing disillusionment with the Soviet model of development and the effects of Moscow's policies of retrenchment and collaboration. Gorbachev's explicit admission that the Soviet system was bankrupt and that the only hope lay through introducing the capitalist market finally crushed the hopes of generations of third world radicals. Furthermore, economic decline resulted in cuts in Moscow's foreign aid budget, forcing, for example, the withdrawal of Cuban troops from southern Africa and Vietnamese forces from Cambodia. By the end of the eighties, the Soviet Union's remaining client regimes were either marginal states (South Yemen, Cuba), or impoverished (Ethiopia, Vietnam), or both (Afghanistan).

Gorbachev's conciliatory diplomatic strategy towards the West meant that the Kremlin used its influence over radical nationalist movements to encourage them into negotiations with the imperialist powers on grossly unfavourable terms. These pressures helped to force Swapo into coming to terms with South Africa in Namibia, the PLO into recognising Israel in 1988, and the ANC into talks with the South African regime, talks which gradually resulted in the abandonment of the objective of black majority rule for the foreseeable future.

The final collapse of the Soviet Union completed the process of disillusionment. The demoralising impact was felt around the world, intensifying the isolation of the handful of defiant nationalist regimes and outstanding liberation struggles. The electoral defeat of governing nationalist movements in Nicaragua and Algeria symbolised the new balance of forces as the West won its revenge for past humiliations. In Ireland, Sinn Fein came under similar pressures to the PLO and the ANC to adopt a more conciliatory approach towards its imperial adversary.

The reversal of Soviet policy towards the Middle East was a key factor in the success of Western strategy in the Gulf War. Forced to fight alone, with at best token support and at worst outright hostility from other third world regimes, Saddam Hussein's regime stood little chance against the New World Order.

Liberal interventionism

The Gulf War also revealed another startling reversal: influential left-wing intellectuals and radical movements in the West, who had long been champions of national liberation in the third world, now took a stand in support of Western intervention.

In fact, despite their past enthusiasm for third world nationalism, most British radicals had never lost their faith in the positive role of the British state. In 1969, many radicals supported the deployment of British troops in Northern Ireland, on the grounds that they would protect the Catholics from pogroms. Still, after 1989, the collapse of the Eastern bloc and the demise of national liberation movements in the third world removed all inhibitions on overt radical support for Western intervention. As a result, the underlying liberal sentiment that the West is a force for progress came to the fore.

In this process the Gulf War was a watershed. Many radicals joined in the mainstream vilification of Saddam Hussein and gave their support to Western military action against Iraq. Even groups which refused to support Operation Desert Storm nevertheless supported the use of Western economic sanctions to bring Saddam Hussein to his knees.

The repression of Kurds in northern Iraq by Saddam Hussein's forces after the Gulf War provoked further radical demands for Western intervention. Many liberals demanded that the West give military protection to the Kurds, and welcomed the establishment of a 'safe haven' in northern Iraq. Some even accused the Western powers of having stopped the Gulf War too soon, before Saddam could be destroyed. The liberals ignored the fact that the Kurdish tragedy was a consequence of the Western-initiated war against Iraq. They also forgot that the Western powers had a long history of suppressing the Kurdish people and that, even as they entered their 'safe haven', the Kurds were still being harassed and killed by the West's local ally, Turkey.

Radical support for Western action against Iraq not only played a key role in permitting the slaughter, it allowed the forces that reduced Iraq to rubble to posture as the standard-bearers of democracy and decency against a despotic third world regime. The result was not merely a spectacular display of military barbarism, but a moral triumph, which paved the way for further Western intervention throughout the world. Since the Gulf War, liberal calls for Western intervention, from Bosnia to Somalia, have become more and more strident.

By the beginning of 1993 the metamorphosis of what had long

regarded itself as a peace movement into a war movement was complete. In a contribution to the continuing debate in the pages of the *New Statesman*—the periodical that had launched Britain's leading peace movement in the 1950s but had now become a staunch advocate of Western intervention—a veteran anti-war activist set about explaining 'the irony that any peace politics can only start now with the use of force':

> A new movement is needed throughout the comfortable West to make sure that the pressure on governments is sustained and unavoidable, and to frame the goals and principles of a new peace politics. It must again link peace with human rights, and embrace a consistent agenda of economic, political and, alas, military intervention. (M Shaw, 'Grasping the nettle', 15 January 1993)

The fact that prominent figures in the erstwhile anti-war movement had redefined peace to mean war gave powerful endorsement to the militarist consensus. It gave the ruling classes of the West a free hand to enforce imperialist policy, under the new guises of bringing 'humanitarian relief', upholding 'human rights' and promoting 'peace processes'.

The impact on Northern Ireland

One indication of rising British confidence in tackling the long-running problem of Northern Ireland was the new intensity of the propaganda barrage against the republican movement—and the breadth of the consensus behind it. For years, the British establishment had sought to minimise domestic support for the Irish cause by depicting its supporters as crazed fanatics gripped by atavistic prejudices, tribal instincts and a proclivity for mindless terrorism. In the early years of the war, such notions were the property of right-wing politicians and pundits. But in recent years, they have been widely assumed by the liberal intelligentsia.

In the development of the imperialist propaganda war, there has been a striking circular relationship between the Anglo-Irish conflict and the wider context of Western-third world tensions. When the Irish

Troubles emerged as a serious problem for Britain in the early seventies, it soon became clear that there was limited scope for the familiar Cold War strategy of branding the nationalist movement as part of the global communist conspiracy to overthrow the Western way of life. For a start the leaders of the 'Provisional' IRA were staunchly anti-communist, even devoutly Catholic, having ousted the Moscow-leaning leadership of the 'Official' republican movement. Furthermore, asserting links between the IRA and national liberation struggles in the third world, at a time when such struggles were attracting mass support in the West, might have enhanced the IRA's legitimacy, rather than undermining it.

Hence Britain's propaganda offensive against the IRA took a quite different tack, but one which was subsequently to acquire wider applicability. Attempts to depict the Provisionals as crypto-communists gave way to the promotion of the view that Irish republicans were motivated by irrational notions rooted deep in their history and psychology, and remote from political or moral constraints. Their loyalty was to an ancient tradition in which they had been initiated by their families (some versions held mother's milk to be the agent of transmission, others blamed the history books). The power of history and of inheritance were also evident in the enduring strength of particular 'tribal' identities, Loyalist as well as republican, and in the use of violence and terror to resolve conflict down the centuries. The familiar themes of 'men of violence', 'evil psychopaths', 'sectarian bloodlust' precluded rationality and justified British interference and military repression.

Much anti-nationalist propaganda was self-evidently absurd: why did these supposedly long-established pathologies only become manifest after 1969? Yet such notions served Britain well in legitimising its civilising role in Ireland during the seventies. After the overthrow of the Shah of Iran in 1979, by a movement which expressed its hostility towards the West in terms of Islamic fundamentalism rather than radical nationalism, many of the familiar anti-IRA themes found a place in the new Western anti-third world ideology. The depiction of national liberation movements (PLO, ANC, Sandinistas in Nicaragua, FMLN in El Salvador) as terrorist conspiracies and radical nationalist regimes (Iran, Libya, Syria) as 'terrorist regimes' came to occupy a central role in Western propaganda.

In the early nineties there was an eruption of new nationalist movements in the former Soviet Union and Eastern Europe, as well as in the third world. Explanations of the conflicts that followed in terms of blood and ethnicity flourished on all sides. In analysing the strife that ravaged the former Yugoslavia from 1991 onwards, British commentators found ready parallels with a familiar conflict closer to home:

> The sheer hate is terrifying. The mutually shared venom that divides the Croatians and the Serbs is something like that which has inspired the slaughter in Northern Ireland for so long; but it is even more acrid and intense, even more deeply steeped in its bloody past—and much better supported by force of arms. (Ed Vulliamy, *Guardian*, 13 January 1992)

If the Irish War now provided a useful set of prejudices through which to interpret post-Cold War conflicts elsewhere, then their wider currency in turn reinforced their application to events in Ireland. Once these notions seemed to acquire a universal validity, then they seemed mere common sense in relation to Ireland too. Another correspondent in the liberal *Guardian* reflected on Ireland at the end of 1991 in terms which would have disgraced the tabloid press 20 years earlier:

> This is a story of an ancient blood feud that stretches back across centuries...in Ireland history does not die. The natives have never forgotten....In Tyrone's green fields men mutter darkly of vendetta, unconsciously plunging between centuries in mid-sentence. (Kevin Toolis, 7 December 1991)

But if all this is true, why were Tyrone's green fields so quiet for half a century before 1969? Had 'the natives' forgotten about their 'ancient blood feud'? And if so, what reminded them of it?

Britain's propaganda war against the Irish republican movement fostered a domestic climate of opinion supportive of the continuation of Britain's civilising role in Ireland. British strategy proceeded along a familiar 'twin track' approach. On the one hand it kept up, and even intensified, the military pressure, raising the oppressive profile of the occupying forces and targeting republicans with 'shoot-to-kill' squads and through collusion with the Loyalist paramilitaries.

On the other hand, in addition to the political initiatives within the framework of the Anglo-Irish agreement, in mid-1990, the British government 'reactivated' its long-dormant 'line of communication' with the republican movement, 'leading to a period of protracted dialogue between Sinn Fein and the British government' ('Setting the record straight', p3).

Mid-1990 was a significant moment for the reopening of secret diplomacy with a movement whose members could not be heard on British television and whose leaders were held in open contempt by all sections of the establishment. The same 'line of communication' had been used during the 1974-75 ceasefires and the 1980-81 hunger strikes, but not since. In mid-1990, however, Eastern Europe had collapsed, but the Soviet Union remained intact, the Gulf War was on the horizon and Margaret Thatcher was still prime minister. Sinn Fein's account of the subsequent contacts, released in January 1994 in response to earlier leaks and misrepresentations by the British government, revealed British officials eager to cultivate the goodwill of leading republicans. Over the next three years, the British cordially encouraged Sinn Fein's 'peace process', indicating divisions within the British cabinet, political difficulties at Westminster and providing advance notice of key ministerial speeches.

The passage quoted at the head of this chapter shows how in September 1993 British representatives secretly urged Sinn Fein to use the Israel/PLO accord as a propaganda device to put public pressure on the British government. In fact, Sinn Fein needed little encouragement to pursue this line. A year earlier, Gerry Adams had stated that 'from South Africa to Palestine, we are witnessing the beginning of what could become processes for the democratic resolution of these conflicts' (*An Phoblacht/Republican News*, 15 October 1992). Martin McGuinness, the key Sinn Fein figure in these secret exchanges, subsequently insisted that the British government should 'learn from South Africa and Israel', and that John Major should 'be radical' in the manner of De Klerk and Rabin and negotiate a settlement (*Guardian Weekend*, 18/19 September 1993).

The striking feature of the way events in South Africa and Palestine were taken up by Sinn Fein leaders was that they perceived the demise of the liberation struggles in these countries as a model for their advance in Ireland. In yet another article in support of the 'peace process' in November 1993, *An Phoblacht/Republican News* summarised its assessment of how international trends pointed in this direction:

> All across the world, direct and indirect dialogue is used as a means to end other seemingly intractable conflicts. Attempts are being made to take the gun out of South African, Palestinian and Salvadorean conflicts. Conflict areas throughout the world are being transformed from theatres of war into political arenas. The blood of battle is being replaced by the passionate dialogue of the political process. (11 November)

It seemed that in their eagerness for dialogue, Sinn Fein leaders were closing their eyes to the realities of the New World Order.

In South Africa, the advance of the 'peace process' following the release of Nelson Mandela from prison in February 1990 coincided with a dramatic increase in violence and bloodshed. Beginning with the massacre at Sebokeng township in July 1990, the conflict has reached the scale of open warfare. Between July 1990 and November 1993, the death toll reached 10 607, with 17 877 wounded, a daily total of more than eight deaths and 15 injuries (Human Rights Commission South Africa, *Human Rights Review,* SR-13). So much for the removal of 'the gun' from the South African conflict.

The carnage in South Africa reflects the government's success in turning the black liberation struggle into a black civil war, in which most violence takes place between ANC supporters and the conservative Inkatha movement. Meanwhile Mandela and the ANC leadership have endorsed an interim 'power-sharing' constitution which institutionalises the divisions within the black majority, while entrenching the power of the white elite (see C Longford, 'Constitutional climbdown', *Living Marxism,* January 1994). So much for a democratic resolution.

In Palestine, in the period of virtually continual 'peace process' between the PLO's recognition of Israel and Yasser Arafat's denunciation of 'terrorism' at the United Nations in 1988 and the handshake between Rabin and Arafat in September 1993, the Intifada raged in the occupied territories. Up to November 1992, this resulted in the deaths of 959 Palestinians and 103 Israelis, with an additional 543 Palestinians killed by fellow Palestinians as collaborators.

Under the terms of the peace agreement clinched in September 1993, Israel would allow limited autonomy to the PLO within the Gaza Strip and the town of Jericho on the West Bank of the River Jordan. For 2.6m refugees (out of a total Palestinian population of 5.8m) the deal promised nothing. For the 13 000 Palestinian political prisoners in Israeli jails there was no amnesty. For Palestinian intellectual Edward Said, the deal was 'an instrument of surrender... a Palestinian Versailles' (*London Review of Books*, October 1993). This surrender brought no end to the bloodshed, or its disproportionate character: in the three months following the historic handshake a further 38 Palestinians were killed, and 18 Israelis (*Guardian*, 13 December 1993).

Surveying peace processes from Angola and Cambodia to Yugoslavia in early 1994, one commentator pointed to the real content of these manoeuvres:

> The true meaning of today's peace process is the opposite of its public image. The peace process is not about reconciling local enemies. It is about pursuing the West's war against the whole of the third world in a new form. The peace process is not about achieving a just settlement to conflicts in Africa or Asia. It is about imposing Western domination around the globe in a more direct fashion. (E Veale, 'Processed peace: don't buy it', *Living Marxism*, No64, February 1994)

When the British government reactivated its line of communication with Sinn Fein, its objective was to pursue a peace process that would integrate the republican movement and stabilise British domination over Ireland.

The endorsement of international peace processes by Sinn Fein leaders reflected the mutual rapport between republican leaders and Mandela and Arafat. Both visited Ireland in the course of 1993 and signalled their approval for Sinn Fein's peace process, gestures warmly welcomed by McGuinness in a speech in Belfast in November (*AP/RN*, 18 November).

In fact there are significant differences between the Irish republican movement on the one hand and the ANC and the PLO on the other. Given the weakness of the left and the strength of Catholic reaction in Ireland, the republican movement never had close ties with the Soviet Union. By contrast the PLO retained links with Moscow to the end and the South African Communist Party is still a powerful force inside the ANC.

The republican movement has never had much support from rich businessmen in the style of the ANC, nor the PLO's backing from Arab regimes and prosperous Palestinian exiles. Donations from Irish America, though a frequent theme of hostile British comment, have never provided a major source of income. Yet, despite its lack of rich sponsors, the IRA has proved a more resilient and resourceful guerrilla movement than the military wings of the ANC or the PLO. The austere lifestyles of Sinn Fein leaders testify to the absence of corruption in the Irish republican movement, compared with other nationalist movements. Numerous British smear campaigns, attempting to link republicans to organised crime, drug-dealing and other rackets, have failed to convince any but those who are already prejudiced against them.

What Sinn Fein shares with the PLO and the ANC is a similar nationalist programme and a tendency to become integrated into existing colonial structures in response to the pressures of isolation. The PLO and the ANC are further down the 'peace process' road because they started out sooner, and because they came under more direct pressure from their erstwhile friends in Moscow. They also faced regimes in deep economic and political crisis which desperately needed to draw their old adversaries into a negotiated solution in the hope that this would bring greater stability. The difficulty facing Sinn Fein has been the greater reluctance of the British government to embark on a potentially risky course of talks after a period of relative stability in Ireland.

One of the forces encouraging the Irish republican movement in the direction of trying to negotiate some new constitutional framework with Britain as a way of resolving the conflict has been the British left. In the early years of the Irish War, the left upheld the demand for Irish national self-determination and campaigned for 'Troops out now'; some even chanted 'Victory to the IRA'. However, once the IRA's bombing campaign in Britain provoked a predictable chauvinist response, the left backed away from giving unconditional support to the anti-imperialist struggle and soon backed away from Irish solidarity activity altogether. Those who remained generally limited their opposition to British rule to condemning particular excesses—such as internment, Bloody Sunday, the use of rubber and plastic bullets, the treatment of prisoners, etc—while campaigning for a more enlightened form of colonial administration. With such a timid and equivocating opposition at home, the British government has long enjoyed a free hand to impose its will in Ireland.

Even before the current peace process got under way, the British left was indicating the way towards some accommodation. At the April 1987 conference of the Labour Committee on Ireland, then an influential Irish solidarity grouping inside the Labour Party, delegates abandoned the demand for 'Troops out now' in favour of a proposal for 'Withdrawal within the lifetime of a Labour government'. By giving a future Labour government the initiative, this position implied that the British state could play a constructive role in Ireland. Furthermore, it made Irish self-determination negotiable, thus negating its substance. Worse still, it made the future of Ireland contingent on the election of a Labour government in Britain. The moderate and conciliatory approach of the mainstream British left towards British domination over Ireland meant that in practice the republican movement remained isolated from any mass support in Britain.

Close links between left-wing Labour activists and Sinn Fein leaders during the eighties encouraged the evolution of republican policy away from national liberation towards the peace process. British radicals—from the Labour left to the old Troops Out Movement—endorsed the advance of the Hume/Adams initiative to its culmination in the Downing Street declaration. The abject response of Geoff Bell, for more than 20 years a leading figure in Irish solidarity circles in Britain, was typical (*Labour Briefing*, February 1994).

Apparently incapable of independent analysis of the declaration, Bell faithfully echoed Sinn Fein demands for clarification and condemned the government for refusing to provide it. Taking the 'peace process' at face value, he accused John Major of a 'cowardly dodge' of the 'great opportunity which now presents itself for peace in Ireland'. He congratulated Sinn Fein on its shift towards compromise, for 'having shown a willingness to be flexible' on the principles of national self-determination. Arguing that 'building a pro-peace campaign...would be a valuable contribution from activists in this country', he concluded that 'the opening of a discussion on organising such a campaign would do no harm at all'. With such a level of passion and commitment among the 'activists', it is not surprising that there is as yet little sign of the discussion, never mind the campaign. Given that any such campaign would merely add to British pressures on the republican movement, the inertia of what remains of the old left is a small mercy.

The peace process appeals to aspirations for an end to 25 years of bloodshed and bitterness, but, as we have seen, it is a cruel deception. A glance around the world at the beginning of 1994 reveals that Western-backed peace deals mean more death and suffering for the peoples of the third world, Eastern Europe—and for the people of Ireland.

3

The twilight of republicanism

In presenting Sinn Fein's initiative 'Towards a lasting peace' to the February 1992 Ard Fheis, president Gerry Adams referred with justification to 'our party, the oldest and most historic revolutionary organisation in this part of the world' (*An Phoblacht/Republican News*, 27 February 1992). Yet the very longevity of the movement reflects its tragic past. The history of Irish republicanism is one of heroic defeats. As the world's oldest liberation struggle, it has a proud record of tenacity and heroism won in desperately uneven combat with the world's first superpower.

The era of struggle for Irish national liberation which opened with the rebellion of the United Irishmen led by Theobald Wolfe Tone in 1798 now appears to be reaching its end. The modern republican movement traces its evolution through the revolts of the nineteenth century, the rising of Robert Emmet in 1803, the Young Ireland Movement of the 1840s and the Fenians of the 1860s. It reached its apogee in the Easter Rising of 1916 and the subsequent War of Independence which culminated in partition in 1920-21.

The phase of nationalist resistance which opened in 1969 has proved the most prolonged and most bloody in the troubled history of relations between imperial Britain and its oldest colony. For nearly a quarter of a century the volunteers of the Irish republican movement have displayed resilience, versatility and courage in fighting what is still one of the world's most powerful armies, and one which has unparalleled experience in counter-insurgency operations. Yet over the past decade, the balance of forces has shifted inexorably in Britain's favour. In the last chapter we looked at the changes in international relations which

45

have strengthened Britain's position in relation to Ireland. Here we focus on developments in Ireland and, in particular, on the Irish republican movement.

Ireland's arrested nationhood is partly the legacy of British domination from the dawn of the capitalist era, which condemned Ireland to a low level of economic and social development. In the nineteenth century the movement for Irish freedom failed to mobilise consistent support from an emerging Irish bourgeoisie too feeble and too compromised with the British ruling class to fight against it, or among a peasantry ground down by famine, poverty and disease.

In the early twentieth century too, Ireland's landowners, manufacturers and traders remained too closely tied to their British colleagues and too divided among themselves to provide consistent support for the national struggle. For them, partition, which allowed Northern industrialists to remain within the markets of the Empire and gave the Dublin elite a degree of autonomy, was a satisfactory compromise. On the other hand, the working class emerged too late and too slowly in a predominantly agricultural country to play a decisive role in the crucial decade from 1910 to 1920. Where the working class was strongest, in the industrial north-east, it was paralysed by sectarian division. Unable to prevent partition, the working class carried the heaviest burden of this terrible defeat for the liberation struggle.

The most important legacy of the failure of the major classes of Irish society to end British domination has been the enhanced role played by the middle classes in Irish politics. Small businessmen, lower-ranking civil servants, professionals and tenant farmers were the driving force behind the movement for Home Rule around the turn of the century. They came to dominate the affairs of the Free State formed in the Twenty-Six Counties in 1921.

Republicanism in its modern form emerged as the ideology of the more radical elements of the Irish middle classes. It advocated independent national development, a project most clearly articulated in the Democratic Programme drawn up in 1919. Proclaiming the principles of 'liberty, equality and justice', the Democratic Programme expressed the aspirations of small businessmen, professionals and tenant farmers for an Ireland in which their enterprises, their careers and their culture could flourish free from British interference. On the character of 'national development' in an independent Ireland, republican policy was always vague, allowing the movement from the outset to include militant socialists and trade unionists as well as small businessmen and farmers. The flexibility of its programme enabled the republican movement to harness the energies of diverse social forces and political tendencies.

The breadth of the republican alliance has also often proved its weakness. The fact that its diverse supporters had different, often contradictory, objectives has made internal division endemic and splits commonplace, particularly at moments when conflict with Britain intensified internal tensions. But, in the absence of any alternative social force capable of pushing the republican movement in a more consistently anti-imperialist direction, the movement has always been vulnerable to the vacillations of the middle classes.

The Irish middle classes aspired towards national independence because of their resentment at the restraints imposed by British rule. At the same time, their reliance on the British state to uphold the capitalist system in Ireland against any challenge from workers in the cities and landless labourers in the countryside set limits on their republican fervour. Torn by these contradictory influences, the middle classes proved incapable of consistently pursuing the national struggle. In times of crisis, they always tended to come to some sort of accommodation with Britain.

The fateful paradox of modern republicanism may be briefly summarised. In the early years of this century, when the working class was a very weak force in Ireland, working class politics was a relatively strong influence on the movement. Over the past two decades, when the working class throughout Ireland has expanded dramatically, it has proved a relatively feeble influence on the republican movement. The result is the continuing ascendancy of a middle class political outlook among the leadership of the republican movement. In the numerous available accounts of the evolution of today's IRA and Sinn Fein, the consequences of this paradox are often overlooked. Most historians emphasise the continuities in the tradition of physical force republicanism, while neglecting the parallel and historically decisive trends towards constitutional nationalism and compromise with the imperial power.

The burden of history

The turbulent decade leading up to partition was a period of strikes and land seizures as well as nationalist revolt. In this climate of intense class struggle and anti-imperialist conflict, one nationalist faction after another made its peace with Britain as layer after layer of the middle classes backed away from the quest for national liberation.

The constitutional nationalist Irish Parliamentary Party, expressing the modest aspirations of the rising Catholic bourgeosie, led the way towards compromise. Its demand for 'Home Rule'—for a devolved administration in Dublin under the authority of the British Crown— was conducted largely through parliamentary manoeuvres at Westminster. When it came to wider social or political issues, the conservatism of Ireland's petty capitalists and larger farmers came to the fore. In 1913, one of its prominent supporters, the entrepreneur William Martin Murphy, instigated a long and bitter lockout of Dublin transport workers in an attempt to crush the growing forces of Irish trade unionism.

On the outbreak of the First World War in 1914, party leader John Redmond declared that the cause of Home Rule could be advanced only by fighting to defend the British Empire in Europe. He called upon the 'Irish volunteers', mobilised to uphold the cause of Home Rule against the threat of Unionist violence, to join the British forces in Europe; tens of thousands went to their deaths in Flanders. When a minority of the volunteers under the leadership of the clandestine Irish Republican Brotherhood joined with James Connolly's workers' militia in the historic Easter Rising in 1916, Redmond and his allies condemned them unreservedly (see CD Greaves, *The Life and Times of James Connolly*, 1976).

However, in the context of the anti-British upsurge that followed the brutal suppression of the Easter Rising, Redmond's support for conscription in the war and his condemnation of the patriot dead of 1916 fatally discredited the Irish Parliamentary Party. The party that had long been the dominant force in the nationalist movement rapidly became a rump.

While Redmond went too soon and stooped too low, Arthur Griffith and Michael Collins, the key signatories of the partition treaty in

December 1921, timed their compromise better. Griffith had founded Sinn Fein in 1905 as an organisation committed to the establishment of a dual British-Irish monarchy along the lines of the Austro-Hungarian empire (a proposal recently revived in various schemes for 'joint sovereignty' over Northern Ireland, with Queens Elizabeth Windsor and Mary Robinson presiding). While more radical republicans supported the workers in the Dublin lockout, Griffith talked of 'having the strikers bayonetted' (P Berresford Ellis, *The Making of the Irish Working Class*, 1985, p197). Although it played no formal role in the Easter Rising, Sinn Fein was the major beneficiary of the wave of popular anti-British outrage that followed the summary execution of the Rising's leaders.

In the November 1918 general election, the last poll to be held in the whole of Ireland, and the first under universal adult suffrage, Sinn Fein won 73 out of 106 seats. Griffith was a leading figure in the independent Dail Eireann (Irish parliament) formed by the Sinn Fein MPs who refused to go to Westminster. Michael Collins, a Cork-born veteran of the Easter Rising, emerged as the commander of the Sinn Fein volunteers, soon to become better known as the Irish Republican Army. Collins became the republican movement's key military strategist in the War of Independence or Tan War (after the 'black and tan' uniform of the British militia) that ensued in 1919 when the British adopted a coercive response to Irish demands for independence.

Between the end of the First World War and partition class conflict raged in Ireland in parallel with the anti-British struggle. The attempt by the British to introduce conscription in April 1918 provoked Ireland's first general strike and a wave of working class militancy. In April 1919, workers in Limerick, inspired by the Bolshevik revolution, proclaimed a 'soviet' and similar initiatives were taken elsewhere (see M Milotte, *Communism in Modern Ireland: The Pursuit of the Workers' Republic Since 1916*, 1984, pp30-34, and L Cahill, *Forgotten Revolution: Limerick Soviet 1919, a Threat to British Power in Ireland*, 1990). By 1920 trade union membership had reached 250 000. In the same period occupations of land, particularly in large estates in the poorer counties, became commonplace. All these initiatives brought militant workers and peasants into conflict with the leadership of the republican movement. In June 1919 the Dail set up the 'republican courts' which clamped down on illegal land seizures and authorised the use of the 'republican police force' to evict landless families (JA Gaughan, *Austin Stack*, pp136-37).

Although the strikes and occupations lacked leadership or organisation, they kept the middle class nationalists under constant pressure. Squeezed between their desire to end British rule and their fear of popular revolt against the capitalist system, they preferred to negotiate a deal with Britain rather than risk social revolution at home. In July 1921 the Sinn Fein leadership consulted with the Dublin establishment, not the Dail or the IRA, before agreeing to a ceasefire pending further negotiations. Once the truce was declared and with the talks continuing in London, the pressure from the respectable classes for a settlement intensified. Irish historian Desmond Greaves comments that 'the chambers of commerce passed their resolutions. Country merchants, cattle dealers, manufacturers great and small took up from their natural superiors, agrarian and financial, the cry for order' (CD Greaves, *Liam Mellowes and the Irish Revolution*, 1971, p270).

In December 1921, the Sinn Fein delegation led by Griffith and Collins signed the Treaty that accepted the partition of Ireland. The new arrangements were rapidly stabilised through sectarian pogroms in the North and civil war between the British-backed Dublin regime and intransigent republicans in the South. Though Griffith died (of natural causes) and Collins was killed (in a Civil War ambush), their fellow representatives of the Irish middle classes were able to take their places in the tawdry Free State regime that was the outcome of this historic defeat of the Irish nationalist movement.

The republican leader who timed his compromise with Britain the most effectively was Eamon de Valera. Spared execution for his role in the Easter Rising by claiming American citizenship, de Valera became a key figure alongside Griffith in the 1919 Dail. He stood aloof from the partition settlement and delayed his capitulation until after the final defeat of the mass anti-British upsurge in the early 1920s. It was not until 1927 that he agreed to take the oath of allegiance to the British Crown—one of the most contentious issues in the Treaty debates—and led his new party, Fianna Fail, into the Free State Dail. Fianna Fail soon became the Free State's natural party of government and de Valera was rewarded with the status of a founding father of the 26-county state.

Partition and the republican movement

As Connolly had predicted back in 1914, when partition had first been mooted as a possible way of resolving the Home Rule crisis, the division of Ireland ushered in a 'carnival of reaction' on both sides of the artificially created border. Just as the Irish economy remained backward, so its social relations stagnated. The working class has remained divided, disorganised and politically ineffectual to this day. The middle classes have continued to dominate political life on both sides of the Border, giving it a distinctively petty and parochial character. Though partition stabilised Ireland as a whole under British rule for half a century, it was only partially successful.

In the South, the Free State regime managed to construct a serviceable national identity and, by the 1960s, even a degree of economic expansion. However, as a result of the early defeat of the nationalist movement and the relative success of the Dublin regime in securing middle class approval over several decades, the nationalist aspirations of the Irish middle classes have today become so attenuated as to have virtually disappeared. In the North, Stormont could only rule by maintaining Loyalist privileges and coercing the substantial nationalist minority. By the 1960s, middle class as well as poor Catholics were seething with resentment.

In the decades following partition, the republican movement suffered repression North and South as it attempted to keep up the struggle for national freedom. Republicans continued to uphold the 1919 Democratic Programme and their commitment to the traditions of physical force. Attempting to overcome their isolation and to broaden their popular appeal, republicans flirted with left-wing politics, in Saor Eire in the late 1920s, in the 1934 Republican Congress, in Clann na Poblachta in the late 1940s and in the Wolfe Tone societies in the 1960s. However, in the absence of a cohesive working class movement, the left acted more as the voice of the radical sections of the middle classes and tended to push the republican movement into a more conciliatory approach towards Britain.

The instability of the left was already apparent in the debates around the Treaty. The labour movement made no attempt to take over the leadership of a flagging national liberation struggle, or to rally the anti-Treaty forces around an anti-imperialist programme. Instead the organisations of the left compounded the prevailing confusion by choosing to follow one or other side in the Civil War. The Irish Labour Party endorsed the Treaty and assumed the title of 'His Majesty's loyal opposition' within the Free State Dail. The tiny Communist Party of Ireland (CPI), formed in 1921, was the first organisation to reject the Treaty. However, instead of taking up an independent anti-imperialist line, it gave its unconditional support to de Valera through the Treaty debates, the Civil War and the subsequent elections. In December 1922, Roddy Connolly, son of James and leading member of the CPI, called upon the IRA to recognise the Free State and to dump arms.

Far from leading the struggle against imperialism from in front, the left whispered its approval for a policy of compromise from the rear, and attempted to give it a radical edge. This subsequently became the familiar role of the left in Irish politics.

In 1934 Roddy Connolly and left republican Mick Price walked out of the Republican Congress, an attempt to link up working class socialists and radical republicans (see G Gilmore, *The Irish Republican Congress*, 1978). The congress had rejected their emphasis on the class struggle and their proposal of the slogan for a 'workers' republic' rather than a 'people's republic'. The 'workers' republic' slogan sounded radical, but when they persuaded the Irish Labour Party to adopt this policy in 1936, it soon became clear that they meant pursuing workers' narrow economic interests within the constraints imposed by a full acceptance of British rule in Ireland. If socialism meant the abandonment of the struggle against Britain, it was not surprising that most Irish republicans did not want to know.

After the Second World War former IRA leader Sean MacBride pulled together the remnants of left republicanism and launched a new party, Clann na Poblachta. This party immediately entered elections, in defiance of Sinn Fein's established practice of refusing to recognise the institutions of the Free State. MacBride soon won a by-election seat in the Dail and his party began to attract growing support. Republican suspicions that Clann na Poblachta would turn out to be just another partitionist party were confirmed after the 1948 election when MacBride's party entered a coalition government with Fine Gael, the party of the original Free Staters, with himself as foreign secretary.

This government's declaration of the Free State as the Republic of Ireland later in the same year ratified the partition of the country against which the republican movement had been fighting for a quarter of a century.

Throughout these years the IRA maintained a military structure and periodically engaged in armed resistance, for example, in the 1939 bombing campaign in England and in the Border campaign in the late 1950s. Yet the republican movement suffered a steady loss of support, particularly in the South, as former activists drifted into mainstream nationalist or socialist organisations.

Intransigent republicans drew the conclusion that engaging in politics, particularly socialist politics, meant betraying the national struggle, and that only by abstaining from politics and relying on the force of arms could the cause of national liberation hope to triumph. J Bowyer Bell aptly sums up the lesson drawn from these bleak decades: 'the *real* republicans put their trust only in physical force and abstentionism from puppet assemblies' (*The Secret Army*, 1979, p243-44). This was a conviction which was to have lasting influence in the republican movement.

Civil rights and republican splits

The distinctive feature of the republican movement of the past two decades is that although its programme has changed little since 1919, its social base has changed utterly. In January 1994, on the seventy-fifth anniversary of the adoption of the Democratic Programme, it was reprinted in full in *An Phoblacht/Republican News* with a commentary emphasising its contemporary relevance (20 January 1994). Yet the republican movement today draws its support from the working class inner-city districts of Northern Ireland and from the poorer rural areas along the Border. Middle class support throughout Ireland has evaporated together with traditional rural backing in the south and west.

Even though the republican movement acquired mass working class support in the North in the 1970s, this has remained largely passive and has failed to exert a distinctive political influence on the direction of the movement. Indeed, instead of encouraging the movement to adopt a new approach appropriate to the new Ireland, the effect of events in the early years of the Troubles was to reinforce the grip of tradition.

In the lean years of the fifties and sixties, a grouping of former members of both the Irish and British official communist movements gained considerable influence within the depleted ranks of the IRA. Under the guidance of intellectuals closely aligned to the Stalinist tradition, the republican movement shifted towards renouncing the two principles which had held it together since the thirties—abstentionism and commitment to the armed struggle.

By the late sixties republicans were getting involved in electoral activity in the South and civil rights agitation in the North. The Northern Ireland Civil Rights Association was launched in January 1967 after a secret meeting between the Wolfe Tone Society, a communist-republican front organisation, and the IRA leadership had agreed on a set of demands to Stormont for the removal of discriminatory measures in elections, housing and for the reform of repressive legislation. The civil rights campaign marked a significant departure from tradition since it implied the reform rather than the destruction of the Stormont state (S Cronin, *Irish Nationalism: A History of Its Roots and Ideology*, 1980, p187). Meanwhile the IRA, anticipating further moves in a more political direction, had got rid of most of its weapons.

Over its first 18 months, the civil rights movement attracted little attention. However in August 1968 a civil rights march from Coalisland to Dungannon, mobilised around a local case of blatant sectarian discrimination in housing, attracted 2500 people and a Loyalist counter-demonstration. The march was blocked by the police. In October a civil rights march in Derry was baton-charged by the RUC and prominent nationalist politicians were brutally beaten. Over the next 12 months confrontations between civil rights marchers and the Stormont state and its Loyalist allies escalated. By August 1969 Northern Ireland had passed out of the control of the Stormont authorities. Riots raged in Belfast and Derry as the RUC, the B-Specials and Loyalist mobs attacked Catholic areas. The British Army was sent in to restore order.

Where in this critical moment was the IRA? This indeed was the question being asked in Catholic areas under Loyalist siege as they turned to their traditional defenders and found them unprepared and lacking the basic weapons and resources to hold off the enemy. The debacle of August 1969 brought long-simmering tensions in the republican movement to a head.

Though the shift of the republican movement away from armed struggle towards electoral politics was provoking growing internal dissension, the leadership around Cathal Goulding and Tomas MacGiolla was determined to push ahead with its emphasis on political campaigning. The evident success of the civil rights strategy encouraged the republican leadership to recommend an end to the abstentionist line at the December army convention.

Meanwhile threatened Catholic areas, particularly in Belfast, were demanding that the IRA release weapons for the defence of the community against Loyalist mobs, the police and, after August, the army. The refusal of the Dublin-based leadership to meet these demands led to growing hostility to its political line. In September, a month after the British occupation, the leaders of the IRA's Belfast brigade once again requested arms from the Dublin headquarters. When their request was again refused they opted to defy the Dublin leadership and set up their own Northern Command. They also demanded the replacement of the IRA chief of staff and the expulsion of a number of prominent left wingers. However their top priority was to build up the virtually non-existent IRA organisation in Belfast and Derry.

The conflict between the political emphasis of the IRA leadership and the military preoccupations of the Northern republicans culminated in a split at the December army convention and the subsequent Sinn Fein conference, when the leadership won a substantial majority for its proposal to abandon abstentionism. Goulding attempted to reassure Northern militants that taking parliamentary seats was merely a matter of tactics and that it implied no retreat from the armed struggle. The object, he later explained, was to 'extend our guerrilla activities and tactics into the very parliament itself' (*New Left Review*, No64, 1970). At a time when the Stormont state was unleashing pogroms against the nationalist communities in the North, many republicans regarded the decision to take seats in this sham parliament as little short of treacherous. They walked out and declared the Provisional republican movement; the old organisation was subsequently known as the Officials.

It is important to recall that at the time this dispute was widely seen as a split between progressive socialists and reactionary republicans. Indeed the Officials emphasised their orientation to the working class, their socialist convictions and their commitment to working in the unions as well as in parliaments. The Provisionals, on the other hand, had little interest in trade unions or elections, recognising that neither had much of a record of protecting Catholics in the North. The Provisionals were vehemently anti-communist, denouncing the Officials for aiming to introduce a 'totalitarian dictatorship' in Ireland. Belfast Provisional leader Jimmy Steele condemned the radical takeover as a 'Red' plot and its leaders as 'the Red infiltrators' (*Republican News,* June 1970). In circumstances where 'communism' meant the betrayal of the anti-imperialist struggle and collaboration in the parliaments of the oppressor, anti-communism was an understandable reaction. The evolution of the rival factions in the split drew out the logic of their positions.

While it retained a formal commitment to the armed struggle in the North, the Official republican movement carried out little military activity. Its best-known actions were the bomb attack on the Parachute Regiment headquarters at Aldershot in February 1972 in retaliation for Bloody Sunday (which killed a chaplain and several women cleaners) and the execution of a young Catholic from Derry who had joined the British Army. In response to the furore generated by the Derry incident, the Officials finally abandoned the armed struggle in May 1972. However, they retained some weapons for use in murderous feuds with both the Provisionals and dissident factions within their own ranks. The Officials evolved into the stridently anti-republican Workers Party which gained some influence in the South in the 1980s. It disintegrated in 1992 following the exposure of its links with both the old IRA and the now defunct Soviet Union.

At the beginning of 1970, the Provisionals had merely a skeleton organisation in Belfast and only a handful of supporters in Derry. However this core of older veterans soon rallied a new generation of republicans. The direct experience of British occupation in the North provided a ready flow of volunteers that soon turned the Provisionals into a highly effective urban guerrilla army. The modern IRA and Sinn Fein are the product of the success of the Provisionals in the North.

When the Provisionals broke from the Officials they rejected the consequences of Stalinism in Ireland but not its politics. They balked at giving up arms and participating in parliaments at a time when the rifle was much more in demand than the ballot box. But the Provisionals never repudiated the broad policy approach that the movement adopted in the sixties. When the Provisionals came to write their own political programme Eire Nua (New Ireland)—published in draft in January 1971 and in a fuller form in June 1972—they based it on a document written by one of the leading Stalinist intellectuals before the split (S Cronin, *Irish Nationalism*, p295). With its call for a democratic socialist republic based on industrial and farming cooperatives, Eire Nua was imbued with the middle class traditions of Irish republican politics. It was the 1919 Democratic Programme expressed in the terms of sixties' reformism and had little relevance to the new working class in the Ireland of the 1970s. However, given the intensity of military conflict in the early seventies, the Provisionals' programme attracted little controversy.

The new generation of republican leaders later regretted the fact that the 1970 split was perceived at the time as conflict between the 'political' Officials and the 'militaristic' Provisionals. This is how Gerry Adams looked back on the failure of the old leadership and the character of the split from the perspective of 1986:

> Understandably in the circumstances, their failure was seen simply in terms of military preparedness, and this view, allied to a suspicion amongst the older republicans of the politicisation process in which the movement was engaged, led to the split in 1970, a major setback for the republican cause. It also ensured that the reinvigorated republican struggle which emerged then was an inadequate one because the only republican organisation which arose from the ashes was a military one: it had little or no proper education process, no formal politicisation courses and there was scant regard paid by the leadership to such needs. (*The Politics of Irish Freedom*, 1986, p35)

Adams' critique of republican strategy in the 1970s justified the leadership challenge from his Belfast faction which in the 1980s once again sought to turn the movement in a more 'political' direction.

The dangers of peace talks

In March 1993, secret talks took place between a British government representative and republican leaders Martin McGuinness and Gerry Kelly in a house near Derry. The Sinn Fein account of this dialogue, released in January 1994, was broadly confirmed by British government sources in a BBC *Panorama* programme in February 1994. The British government representative asserted that Britain now accepted that a united Ireland was inevitable: 'Unionists will have to change. This island will be as one' ('Setting the record straight', p28). Furthermore, he indicated that if the IRA agreed to a two-week suspension of military activities, high-level talks could take place immediately: he had been instructed 'to inform Sinn Fein that if this was agreed at six o'clock, that clearance for meetings at the level of delegations would be forthcoming by one minute past six'. Impressed that British policy had shifted towards disengagement from Ireland, the republican leaders secured IRA agreement on a temporary ceasefire.

In the event, the British government snubbed the republican initiative. No doubt the climate created by IRA bombs at Warrington in March and Bishopsgate in April was not conducive to the opening of talks with Sinn Fein. The government was also preoccupied by the problems of getting the Maastricht treaty through the House of Commons, for which it required the support of Unionists who would be hostile to such a step. There could be little doubt, however, that the British government was heartened by the revelation that the republican movement was prepared to declare a truce, even temporarily, in return for talks. The government could bide its time.

The March 1993 meeting contained another striking exchange. Evidently aware of republican suspicions, the British government representative went out of his way to reassure them: 'British government is sincere. No cheating involved.' He specifically distinguished the government's attitude on this occasion with its approach to the 1975 truce talks, quoting a letter from Northern Ireland secretary Merlyn Rees to Labour prime minister Harold Wilson: 'We set out to con them and we did', ('Setting the record straight', p28). The positive response of the republican delegation to the British representative's proposals suggests that these reassurances were, at least to some extent, successful.

A look back at earlier attempts to negotiate a settlement—in 1972 as well as 1975—suggests that the British government may well have been following a similar strategy in 1993. These episodes revealed serious political weaknesses in the republican leadership, which were again exposed in the above exchanges. Republicans have consistently misassessed the British government's willingness to talk as a sign of readiness for withdrawal. In 1975 they were indeed 'conned' into suspending the armed struggle for a prolonged period by ministers' hints that Britain was seriously considering disengagement. They have also underestimated the dangers of talks in disorienting the movement and fomenting internal conflicts. These weaknesses have been skilfully exploited by the British to the detriment of the national struggle.

In June 1972, following informal contacts between the Provisional IRA and the British government, via SDLP leader John Hume, the Provisionals called an indefinite truce pending full-scale negotiations on 'ending hostilities altogether' (S MacStiofain, *Memoirs of a Revolutionary*, 1975, p266). In July, a republican delegation, including chief of staff Sean MacStiofain, Daithi O'Connell, Gerry Adams—specially released from prison—and Martin McGuinness, was flown to London for talks with home secretary William Whitelaw. However, while the discussions were inconclusive, two days after the London meeting a gun battle in West Belfast brought the truce to a precipitate end. Recognising how the truce had damaged the reputation of the IRA in the nationalist community, MacStiofain later admitted that the republican leadership was forced to call it off when 'it knew it could not hold back any longer' (*Memoirs of a Revolutionary*, p288-89).

The British had welcomed the IRA's ceasefire as an indication of the pressure of war weariness in the nationalist community and as an opportunity to stir up trouble within the republican ranks. Shortly after the breakdown of the truce, the *Financial Times* noted that the British government was hopeful of influencing the more moderate republican leaders at the expense of those they regarded as the military hardliners: 'Some ministers were not too depressed by the attitude displayed by the team's leader, O'Connell. They also see Rory O'Brady and even Joe Cahill as possible "men of reason". (15 July 1972) Whether or not this was an accurate interpretation of the differences in the republican leadership, it indicated the direction of British strategy.

At the time, however, the truce and the recognition given to the IRA leaders by the British government inspired illusions among the republican leaders about the prospect of major British concessions. On the day after the IRA had declared its indefinite truce, Sinn Fein issued its full Eire Nua programme, declaring that 'the possibilities of creating a New Ireland were never greater' (R O'Brady, *Our People, Our Future*, 1973, p21). Meanwhile Whitelaw told parliament that his first priority was to destroy the IRA and before the end of July, Operation Motorman, the biggest military initiative of the Irish War, set out to do just that. Within hours the barricades that had defined 'no-go areas' for troops were swept aside and British soldiers were in control of the whole of occupied Ireland. Motorman marked the beginning of a period of more house searches, arrests, beatings and interrogations.

Taken together, the truce, the talks and Motorman marked a major setback for the republican movement. A sympathetic account conceded that in 1973 'mass support for the IRA within the minority community was...at its lowest ebb since the war began' (K Kelley, *The Longest War: Northern Ireland and the IRA*, 1982, p199). Though the IRA rallied its forces, the republican leadership continued to underestimate the commitment of the British state to the occupation of Northern Ireland. For example, in April 1974 an editorial in *An Phoblacht* was headed 'Brits get ready to pull out' (19 April). Such misjudgments were to have even more serious consequences when, in 1974, the new Labour government launched the most sophisticated attempt so far to crush the republican movement.

The interlinked policies of 'Ulsterisation' meant replacing British soldiers with 'Ulster' policemen, treating freedom fighters like common criminals in the courts and the prisons, and setting up political structures to give the impression, at least in Britain and abroad, that people in Northern Ireland could participate democratically in British rule. Talks with the republican leaders and a prolonged truce played a key role in paving the way for the Ulsterisation strategy.

In December 1974 leading republicans were invited to meet

prominent Northern Ireland churchmen at Feakle in County Clare. As two of the participants later explained, God's work was in remarkable alignment with the requirements of British policy:

> It became clear that there were "hawks" and "doves" in the [IRA] Army Council....Our strategy was to try to strengthen the "doves". There were clearly those who inclined to the view that it would at that juncture be right to call a ceasefire and "go political". (E Gallagher and S Worrall, *Christians in Ulster 1968-1980*, p97)

An indefinite ceasefire came into effect in February 1975. Based on substantial concessions regarding prisoners, internment, withdrawing troops to barracks and scaling down arrests and stop and search procedures, as well as the establishment of 'incident centres' manned by Sinn Fein, the truce lasted for nearly 12 months.

The key factor in the IRA leadership's agreement to suspend the armed struggle was the success of the British representatives in convincing the republicans that the truce was merely the first step down the road towards British disengagement. O'Connell later revealed that the Provisionals and the Labour government had talked repeatedly during the truce about 'devising measures of British disengagement from Ireland' (*Irish Times*, 21 July 1983). An account based on interviews with civil servants at the Northern Ireland Office confirms that the British authorities pursued a deliberate strategy of giving the republican leaders the impression that withdrawal was imminent (see P Bew and H Patterson, *The British State and the Ulster Crisis: From Wilson to Thatcher*). In fact the British never had the slightest intention of pulling out: talk of withdrawal was simply a ruse to extract concessions from republican leaders and sow confusion in the ranks. A colleague observed that the waffling style of Northern Ireland minister Merlyn Rees was a 'major virtue' at a time when 'obfuscation was central to state policy' (*The British State and the Ulster Crisis*, p87).

The 'incident centres', indicating British recognition of the authority of the IRA in nationalist areas, were crucial to British strategy in the truce. Though the new legitimacy conferred on the republican movement alarmed the SDLP and the Dublin government, the British considered that this was a small price to pay for getting the IRA to police the ceasefire and for encouraging republicans to abandon the armed struggle in favour of community politics. According to Desmond Hamill, an author with access to Army sources, the centres were 'all part of a deliberate policy of politicising the Provisionals, and aimed at the long-term stability of the province' (*Pig in the Middle: The Army in Northern Ireland*, 1985, p176-77).

Even before the truce began, one republican expressed his scepticism about the terms of the proposed ceasefire: 'Suppose we get the release of all detainees, an amnesty and withdrawal of troops to barracks, we are still back where we started in 1969.' (*Sunday Times*, 19 January 1975) Once the ceasefire had been agreed and the incident centres established, disaffection spread. In summer 1975 it reached a head over the republican leadership's proposal to replace the annual internment commemoration with a 'festival', though in the event a major riot disrupted plans for the weekend.

In November 1975 Rees announced that the incident centres would close down. They had allowed the British authorities to contain the republican movement and to build up comprehensive intelligence on the IRA in the key nationalist areas. The ceasefire dragged on for another few weeks before breaking down early in 1976. The definitive end of the truce came in March 1976 when the Army raided the Sinn Fein headquarters on the Falls Road in West Belfast and the government withdrew political status from republican prisoners of war.

The impact of the truce on the anti-imperialist struggle was catastrophic. Some years later, Gerry Adams admitted that the republican movement had come close to defeat during the truce:

> The wind-down of the IRA's armed struggle allowed the British to introduce criminalisation against the most confused background possible. They were able to withdraw some regular Army units, transfer more duties to the RUC and UDR and probably came nearer at that time to defeating the republican struggle than at any time during the last 14 years. (*AP/RN*, 21 July 1983)

At the time, however, republican leaders were still anticipating an early withdrawal. As late as November 1975 O'Brady told Sinn Fein supporters that 'we shall win, because we regard British disengagement from

Ireland now as inevitable' (*An Phoblacht*, 7 November 1975).

The key factor in preventing the success of Ulsterisation was the reorganisation of the IRA and its return to active resistance. 'The resumption of military struggle by the IRA prevented the successful implementation of their timetable', wrote Adams in his later account (*The Politics of Irish Freedom*, 1986, p101). In 1977 and 1978 the IRA was reorganised from a battalion to a cell structure in a drive to raise morale and limit the damage resulting from the activities of informers and British intelligence.

The fact that the reassertion of the commitment to the armed struggle had once again rescued the republican movement from the consequences of its political strategy reinforced traditional prejudices against 'politics'. It also meant that the political weaknesses exposed in the truces were never acknowledged and tackled. In the decade after the 1975 truce the leadership around MacStiofain, O'Brady and O'Connell was gradually elbowed aside by the younger generation of Northern republicans—Adams and McGuinness, Danny Morrison, Tom Hartley, Jim Gibney and Joe Austin. Though the old leadership lost considerable authority as a result of its responsibility for the truce, it was never called to account politically. Indeed the slowness of the takeover reflects the considerable degree of continuity between the two leadership factions.

However, the Northern activists increasingly acknowledged that the military struggle could not, on its own, defeat the British and emphasised the need for a broader political campaign, with a radical appeal throughout Ireland. This change in direction was signalled in the annual Bodenstown address in 1977, delivered by Jimmy Drumm:

> The isolation of socialist republicans around the armed struggle is dangerous and has produced the reformist notion that "Ulster" alone is the issue, without the mobilisation of the working class in the Twenty-Six Counties....
>
> We find that a successful war of liberation cannot be fought exclusively on the backs of the oppressed in the Six Counties, nor around the physical presence of the British Army. (*Republican News*, 15 June 1977)

To see how the turn of the republican movement in what appeared to be a more left-wing (and South-facing) direction culminated in today's 'peace process' we need to examine the evolution of republican policy in the eighties.

The exhaustion of republicanism

'There can be peace in '93'—the New Year headline in *AP/RN* heralded the 12 months in which Gerry Adams entered the prolonged dialogue with John Hume that paved the way for the Joint Declaration by John Major and Albert Reynolds. The headline stood in dramatic contrast to the 'Year of victory' proclamations of two decades earlier. Its message was made all the more potent by the backpage endorsement of 'the path of peace' in an official statement by the leadership of the IRA. After more than 20 years of resistance, the republican movement declared its readiness to negotiate a settlement.

To grasp the dynamic of this process it is useful to focus on two key republican conferences. The first is the October 1986 Ard Fheis at which Sinn Fein voted to abandon the long-standing policy of abstentionism in the Twenty-Six Counties. The decision that republicans would, if elected, take their seats in the Dail implied acceptance, for the first time, of the legitimacy of the Dublin regime. Abstentionism continued in the North: Gerry Adams refused to attend at Westminster following his election as MP for West Belfast in 1983 and 1987. The second is the February 1992 Ard Fheis at which Sinn Fein adopted 'Towards a lasting peace' and embarked on the current 'peace process'.

A decade after the ceasefire debacle of the mid-seventies, the republican movement appeared once again to have reached an impasse on both military and political fronts. The new Northern leadership, now confident in its control over the movement, sought to move forward by achieving a more subtle balance between the 'Armalite' and 'the ballot paper', in the terms made famous by Danny Morrison at the 1981 Ard Fheis. The new shift involved a more careful and selective approach by the IRA, with more targeting of British soldiers, less town centre bombings and, hopefully, fewer civilian casualties. It also involved a greater emphasis on political campaigning, in elections and around community issues, particularly in the South, as a way of breaking out of the deadlock in the North.

The abstentionist policy appeared to be a barrier to political advance in the Twenty-Six Counties and the leadership resolved to remove it at the 1986 Ard Fheis. In his keynote address, Gerry Adams insisted that the development of a '32-county wide political struggle' was the most important task facing the movement, emphasising 'projects of economic, social or cultural resistance' (*The Politics of Revolution: Main Speeches and Debates from the 1986 Ard Fheis,* p11). Acutely aware of the ghosts of the past, Sinn Fein leaders repeatedly reassured activists that there would be no retreat from the armed struggle. Indeed they bolstered their position by securing prior endorsement of their policy to end abstentionism from a General Army Convention of the IRA—the first since 1970. The overwhelming vote in favour of the leadership line was the outcome of a series of events in the preceding years.

The 1980-81 H-Block hunger-strikes, in which 10 republican prisoners died demanding political status from a ruthless British government, played a key role in pushing the republican movement further into the political arena. The very fact that the prisoners of war became the central focus of the struggle from the late seventies onwards reflected the defensive posture of the movement. Yet popular hostility towards British intransigence throughout Ireland and beyond provoked mass demonstrations of sympathy and support. Bobby Sands, the first hunger-striker to die won a historic by-election victory at Fermanagh and South Tyrone. The viability of entering the electoral sphere was confirmed when Sands' election agent held his seat following his death and two hunger-strikers were elected to the Dail.

Sinn Fein's electoral interventions in the aftermath of the hunger-strikes brought further encouraging results. In the election to the newly established Ulster Assembly in 1982, Sinn Fein candidates (still on an abstentionist ticket) won 10 per cent of the votes and five seats. In the 1983 Westminster general election, Adams won West Belfast and Morrison narrowly missed election in mid-Ulster. In May 1985, Sinn Fein ran candidates in council elections in Northern Ireland—candidates who for the first time since the early twenties agreed to take their seats if elected. Following the polls, some 59 Sinn Fein councillors took office, and in Omagh and Fermanagh Sinn Fein won the council chairs. The subsequent Unionist boycotts of council meetings reduced local government to a shambles.

Sinn Fein's election successes were a heavy blow to the British propaganda machine which had long tried to depict the republican movement as a terrorist conspiracy without popular backing among the nationalist people. The consistency of the Sinn Fein vote in the Assembly, Westminster and local council elections also confirmed that support for the republican movement was no mere burst of sympathy for the hunger-strikers. The various polls taken together indicated a base of support for Sinn Fein amounting to about 12 per cent of the electorate in Northern Ireland and more than one third of the nationalist community.

Could Sinn Fein supplant the SDLP, the mainstream Catholic nationalist party in the North? In the mid-eighties, this question remained unresolved. Undoubtedly Sinn Fein's early election successes were a shock to the SDLP, yet John Hume's triumph over Morrison in the 1984 European election had helped to reassure his party—and its ardent supporters in Dublin and London. Furthermore, Sinn Fein's high hopes in the 1985 local elections in the North had not been fulfilled, as the SDLP held its own. In by-elections in January 1986, the SDLP vote increased, while Sinn Fein's declined.

There were indications that, to a degree, Sinn Fein and the SDLP appealed to different constituencies. Sinn Fein won votes from lower paid or unemployed nationalists in West Belfast and Derry and in the rural areas along the Border, where the republican movement had mobilised young people and traditional supporters who previously scorned the polling booths. The SDLP retained its support among the more upwardly mobile Catholics in the more respectable nationalist areas.

Could Sinn Fein, as distinct from H-Block hunger-strikers, win seats in the South? Before the 1986 Ard Fheis, this big question remained untested, but with an MP eligible to go to Westminster and dozens of councillors, the leadership had grounds for optimism.

Another important influence on the drive to abandon abstentionism was the Anglo-Irish Agreement signed by Margaret Thatcher and Garret FitzGerald at Hillsborough Castle outside Belfast in November 1985. The main features of the agreement were the establishment of a consultative forum in which British ministers discuss the affairs of the North with members of the Dublin government and agreement on tighter cross-border collaboration in policing the republican movement. The agreement had a limited effect in bolstering the SDLP against Sinn Fein's electoral advance. However, the most important consequence of the agreement, partly obscured by vociferous Unionist posturing against it, was its role in reinforcing an anti-republican consensus, particularly in the South.

The apparent popularity of the agreement in the South underlined the fact that most people in the 26-county state had come to accept the Dublin government as legitimate. The agreement reinforced the combination of censorship and propaganda that served to confine the modern republican movement to the North. For the Sinn Fein leadership, getting rid of abstentionism seemed a pragmatic first step towards breaking out of its isolation in the North and challenging the London-Dublin drive to marginalise the movement throughout Ireland.

Abstentionism remained a highly sensitive issue. Since partition, the hard core of the republican movement had come to define itself by its intransigent refusal to recognise the institutions imposed on Ireland, North and South, by Britain. As we have seen, in most of the major disputes that have divided the movement in subsequent decades, the issue of recognising the framework of British domination has come to the fore as a symbol of the tendency towards compromise. Though the compromisers—de Valera, MacBride, MacGiolla/Goulding—sought first to sway the republican movement from its abstentionist line, the matter of carrying on the armed struggle against British domination was invariably closely related. All the factions that split away from the republican movement sooner or later agreed to lay down arms—unless they were required for use against intransigent republicans. However, given the continuing brutality of the British military occupation of the North and the historic commitment of the Irish republican movement to oust the British by force of arms, the compromisers have always preferred to challenge the movement on the constitutional issue of abandoning abstentionism, rather than openly proposing the abandonment of the armed struggle.

All the proponents of abandoning abstentionism prefaced their arguments with declarations that the armed struggle must continue. Joe Austin, a prominent Belfast radical, insisted that 'the old taboos of the militaristic leadership, that electoral intervention would lead to constitutional sell out, have gone' (*Workers' Press*, 13 September 1986). In response, traditionalists insisted on the link between going political and dumping arms. 'Dropping abstentionism would be as unthinkable as the IRA discussing the surrender of arms', declared O'Brady, leading the rearguard resistance to Adams' proposals (*Times*, 26 September 1986).

As a result of long and careful preparation, the leadership carried the vast bulk of the movement behind the new policy. O'Brady and O'Connell walked out, but their influence had long been in decline and they rallied few under their new banner of Republican Sinn Fein. It was significant that their supporters tended to be among an older genera-tion, mainly in the South; the crucial Northern heartlands—and the IRA—remained solidly behind Adams.

The 1986 Ard Fheis, however, offered two hostages to fortune. In his cautious advocacy of electioneering in the South, Adams warned against expecting quick results: it would only be at the election follow-ing the next one that activists could expect to make significant progress. The veteran Belfast republican Joe Cahill offered crucial endorsement to the Adams strategy from the generation that founded the Provisionals. He reassured delegates about Adams' time-scale, claiming that by that time 'the freedom fighters of the IRA would have forced the Brits to the conference table' (*The Politics of Revolution*, p22). Such statements no doubt received widespread approval among the rank and file. But what when the election after next had come and gone and Sinn Fein had still failed to make headway in the South and the IRA had yet to force the Brits to talk? By the early 1990s, these questions could no longer be dodged.

The path towards the peace process

The republican movement met in Dublin in the last week of February 1992 at the close of a month of grim events that indicated the intense pressures bearing down on the nationalist community in the North.

● 4 February: A crazed RUC officer stormed into the Sinn Fein office in Falls Road, Belfast and opened fire, killing three people and injuring several more; the RUC man subsequently shot himself.

● 5 February: The Loyalist paramilitary UFF shot dead eight Catholics in a random sectarian attack on a betting shop in Ormeau Road, Belfast.

● 16 February: Four IRA men, the eldest 22, killed in an ambush by the SAS at Clonoe, Tyrone; another IRA man died in a similar attack in Fermanagh a week earlier.

● 17 February: The renegade republican group IPLO murdered a Protestant youth in a random sectarian attack in Belfast.

After more than 20 years of war, there appeared to be no end to the bloodshed and the suffering. The British response to the upsurge in violence was to order an extra 600 troops into the North, which could only increase the repression of the nationalist community still further.

The increase in Loyalist terror, which claimed a total of 13 Catholic lives in February, followed the conviction of British agent Brian Nelson. As a senior officer in the Ulster Defence Association, Nelson had been involved in numerous sectarian killings as well as in importing arms from South Africa for the use of the Loyalist paramilitaries. Despite the best efforts of the judiciary, the trial confirmed the extent of collusion between British intelligence and Loyalist paramilitaries. Later in the month, RUC officers visited Sinn Fein activists in Belfast to inform them that their files had been passed on to the death squads: between January 1990 and June 1993 some 13 Sinn Fein members were murdered by Loyalists.

The ruthless use of shoot-to-kill squads against IRA units continued to inflict heavy setbacks. In May 1987 at Loughgall in Armagh, eight volunteers were summarily executed in an SAS ambush. In a similar operation in March 1988 in Gibraltar, three volunteers—including former Armagh women's prison leader Mairead Farrell—were shot dead. In June 1991 a British death squad killed a further three volunteers in Coagh, Tyrone.

After its successes in the eighties, Sinn Fein too had been pushed back on the defensive. Though Adams held his West Belfast seat with an increased majority in the Westminster election in 1987, Sinn Fein won a disappointing 1.9 per cent of the poll in the South in the same year.

More seriously in view of Adams' hopes at the 1986 Ard Fheis of a breakthrough at the election after next, in the June 1989 elections to the Dail, Sinn Fein's share of the vote dropped to 1.2 per cent.

A series of anti-republican propaganda initiatives aiming to intensify the isolation of the movement was assiduously promoted by the British government, their local allies and the media. These included campaigns such as Families Against Intimidation and Terror, protesting against IRA punishment shootings of criminals, and various 'peace campaigns'. Though these projects made little headway in the North, they contributed to a general decline in morale. The sectarian attacks on Protestants by the IPLO, another breakdown product of the old Official movement via the Irish National Liberation Army (INLA), indicated a dangerous tendency towards fragmentation and degeneration in the republican ranks. Such incidents were vehemently condemned by Sinn Fein as a violation of republican traditions and a propaganda gift to the British: the IPLO was finally suppressed by the IRA in November 1992. In the meantime, its actions contributed to a pervasive war-weariness.

The very circumstances of the 1992 Ard Fheis reflected the convergence of the forces seeking to marginalise the republican movement. Banned by the Dublin authorities from its customary venue—the historic Mansion House, seat of the first Dail of 1919—Sinn Fein faced a concerted campaign to drive the Ard Fheis out of Dublin. In the event, despite harassment from the Garda Special Branch and pickets from the virulently anti-republican New Consensus, the conference was finally held in a community centre in the Ballyfermot estate. (In 1993 the republican movement was forced to make the symbolic retreat from Dublin to the Border town of Dundalk to hold its conference.)

The unanimous endorsement of the document 'Towards a lasting peace' at the Ard Fheis confirmed the lowering of republican horizons in response to the pressures of repression and isolation. In his presidential address, Adams affirmed the movement's readiness 'to talk to anyone without preconditions' (*AP/RN*, 27 February 1992). Much of Adams' speech was taken up with reassurances to the Unionists, and indications of the republican movement's readiness to soften its demand for national self-determination. In a speech that was regarded by the British authorities as even more significant because of his close association with the IRA, Martin McGuinness echoed Adams' line.

'We are quite prepared', he declared, 'to be open and flexible to serious proposals which can lead to a realistic settlement'. The message received by the British government was that the republican movement was ready to make real concessions in return for the involvement of Sinn Fein in 'inclusive dialogue'.

Though there was much common ground between 'Scenario for peace' adopted at the 1987 Ard Fheis and the 1992 document, there was a significantly more conciliatory tone in the conference discussion. 'Scenario for peace' significantly proposed that 'a cessation of all offensive actions by all organisations would create the climate necessary for a peaceful transition to a peaceful settlement'. Yet it also insisted that 'a definite date within the lifetime of a British government would need to be set for the completion of...withdrawal'. 'Towards a lasting peace' emphasises dialogue and 'democratic resolution', rather than 'withdrawal' and sets no time limits. Both documents assumed that the British state could—and should—play a constructive role in facilitating the transition to a peaceful Ireland.

The adoption of 'Scenario for peace' in 1987 signalled a more conciliatory approach, not only towards Britain, but also towards the SDLP. During the hunger-strikes and the subsequent electoral contests, Sinn Fein activists had denounced the SDLP as right-wing and middle class, as well as accommodating towards Britain. In the more conservative climate of the late eighties, Sinn Fein leaders sought to retreat from what they regarded as a 'leftist'—or even 'ultra-leftist'—stance, in favour of emphasising their common nationalist outlook. In 1988 Adams entered a prolonged dialogue with Hume, while also issuing a wider call for a 'national consensus' on Irish reunification, appealing to Fianna Fail in the South as well as the SDLP in the North.

Though the 1988 Adams-Hume talks broke down over Sinn Fein's refusal to abandon the traditional republican commitment to national self-determination, the drift towards respectability was clear. When the 1992 Ard Fheis adopted 'Towards a lasting peace' and Adams signalled a willingness to fudge on national self-determination, the way was open for the new round of talks between Adams and Hume that culminated in the 1993 'peace process'.

Subsequent political developments encouraged the evolution of the 'peace process' launched in February 1992. At the Westminster election in April, Adams lost his West Belfast seat to SDLP candidate Joe Hendron. Though this was largely the result of tactical voting by Unionists in a reorganised constituency, with some assistance from SDLP malpractice subsequently endorsed by the judiciary, it was a symbolic blow to Sinn Fein and a boost to the SDLP. Sinn Fein's ill-advised anticipation of a Labour victory in Britain also ended in disappointment at the return of the Tories and the appointment to the Northern Ireland Office of what they considered as a 'hardline' team under Patrick Mayhew. Even worse was the outcome of the November election in the South, in which Sinn Fein won 1.7 per cent of the vote, confirming its marginalisation in the area that had been identified as the key to advance over the previous decade.

What were the implications of the 'peace process' for the armed struggle? As we noted in the context of the abstentionism debate, the inherent tension in the 'Armalite' and 'ballot paper' strategy was acknowledged from the outset. Competition for scarce resources—for funds and competent personnel—is inevitable. The arrival of a substantial cache of arms from Libya in the mid-eighties allowed the leadership of the republican movement temporarily to overcome the difficulties. Indeed for a period, the inherent contradictions of the abstentionism debate were suspended as the IRA stepped up its military activities in parallel with the rising political profile of Sinn Fein. However, by the late eighties, the Libyan connection was broken, the British forces inflicted serious setbacks on the IRA, and the old conflict between the armed struggle and politics inevitably resurfaced.

There is an inescapable conflict between trying to broaden the movement's electoral appeal while waging a military campaign that will inevitably be branded as terroristic and always carries the risk of civilian casualties. The explosion of a massive bomb in Bishopsgate in the City of London on the same day in April 1993 that the Adams-Hume peace talks became public inevitably gave the impression that the two strands of republican policy were not running in parallel, but in conflict. However, the continuing need to defend the nationalist community in the North against British and Loyalist attack has made it difficult for the republican movement to give up its arms.

The attempt to pursue a more selective military strategy since the late eighties has not been particularly successful. The conditions of intense military surveillance and constant Loyalist menace make modern guerrilla war in what is a very small territory particularly diffi-cult. The killing of 11 Protestant civilians in the Remembrance Day bombing at Enniskillen in November 1987 was a characteristic disaster. Such incidents intensified sectarian animosities, handed a propaganda gift to the enemy and put the nationalist community even more on the defensive. 'You have to be careful and careful again', Adams warned the IRA publicly at the 1989 Ard Fheis, in what became a familiar theme.

In the early nineties, even tighter British repression made it more difficult for the IRA to maintain a selective campaign. It undoubtedly scored some impressive successes—the two massive bombs in the City of London in April 1992 and April 1993 were a serious blow to British confidence and imposed heavy costs on the British state. The campaign against British bases along the border, using mortars, remote control bombs, snipers and a variety of other tactics has inflicted heavy losses and imposed major costs on the occupying forces.

Yet such successes have often been obscured by disasters, such as the deaths of two boys in Warrington in March 1993 or the killing of eight Protestant civilians in the Shankill bombing in October 1993. Such high-risk operations provide a propaganda gift to the authorities and have a demoralising effect on the nationalist community. The return to large-scale bombings of shopping centres and other urban areas in the North also gives the propaganda advantage to the British. Bomb attacks on predominantly Protestant towns like Craigavon, Bangor, Newtonards, Coleraine—or even a village like Markethill, which was virtually destroyed by a 1000lb bomb in August 1991—are easily depicted as sectarian, and they are certainly more disruptive and dangerous for ordinary people than they are for the British state. When it comes to killings of workers engaged on security force contracts, which have reached 30 since 1985, including eight Protestants blown up in a works van at Teebane Cross, County Tyrone, in January 1992, the distinction between sectarian and legitimate targets is difficult for most nationalists to accept, never mind Unionists.

The big bombs in the City have been accompanied by dozens of smaller bombs in London and elsewhere, deployed in an apparently random and purposeless way. Such bombs risk the lives of ordinary people without putting any pressure on the British government or raising any awareness of the issue of Irish freedom (see M Kennedy, 'Bomb warnings', *Living Marxism*, December 1992).

The key problem of the IRA's military campaign is that Sinn Fein's peace process has deprived it of any rationality. For the last 20 years and more the armed struggle had a clear role in the wider struggle for Irish freedom. It was necessary to defend the nationalist community, to weaken the British state—in Ireland, in Britain, elsewhere—and to advance the project of national independence and unity. But now the republican movement has proclaimed that it is no longer aiming to drive the British out of Ireland, but seeks recognition in an inclusive dialogue of reconciliation. In these circumstances, the armed struggle is at best a tactic subordinate to the wider peace process, seeking merely to strengthen the negotiating position of the republican representatives. At worst, it sometimes seems that the main purpose of IRA military activities is to protect the leaders of the republican movement against the accusation that they have abandoned the cause of Irish freedom.

The dangers of opportunism

The higher profile of Sinn Fein in recent years has focused growing attention on the politics of the republican movement. We have so far concentrated on its policies and practice in relation to the central issue of Irish society—the national question. What else does Sinn Fein stand for? This is how Adams summed up the aims of the movement in a speech to a Dublin audience in August 1993:

> Our long-term goal is for a 32-county, democratic, socialist republic based upon the 1916 Proclamation. We would like to see a system of decentralised economic and political structures in a pluralist, non-sexist Ireland. (*AP/RN*, 19 August 1993)

In this way Adams seeks to link the traditions of 1916 to the preoccupations of the trendy intelligentsia of modern Ireland. But how, in reality, can a new Ireland be based on a leaflet hastily written more than 75 years ago?

If we turn to Sinn Fein's manifestos for recent elections for further clarification of party policy, we find much in common with those of a traditional social-democratic party. The most striking feature is that, in common with such parties across the world in recent years, all mention of the term 'socialism' has suddenly disappeared. In this respect, Adams' speech lags behind Sinn Fein policy development. In other respects, the manifestos read like old British Labour Party conference documents, with bland appeals for 'democratic economic planning', for an 'integrated economic strategy' or for 'a democratic economy'. Sinn Fein opposes low pay, health and welfare cuts and supports a better deal for the disabled, the elderly and lone parents. Who could disagree?

Adams would like to see a 'pluralist, non-sexist Ireland'. How then does Sinn Fein approach two areas of great importance in Irish politics—the Church and women's rights? Founded by a Presbyterian (Wolfe Tone) and supported at every stage in its evolution by dissident Protestants, the republican movement has long declared its commitment to a secular Ireland. Yet its reliance on a nationalist people strongly influenced by Catholicism has frequently led the republican movement into making concessions to religious reaction.

For example, Sinn Fein's programme includes no demand for a separation of Church and state and no proposal for the removal of schools from clerics, an issue of great importance where priests, brothers and nuns continue to exercise enormous influence over education. It is also noteworthy that, whereas in the past the republican movement could always point to prominent Protestants in its ranks, today such individuals are a rarity. By contrast, leading republicans today feel little reticence about making public displays of Catholic devotion.

The consequences of the republican movement's deference towards the Church are most clearly evident in its opportunism on the question of women's rights. In the eighties, two constitutional amendments ratified the oppression of women in Irish society. A national referendum in 1983 voted by a large majority to make Ireland's ban on abortion part of the Free State constitution and again in 1986 an even bigger majority voted against removing the ban on divorce that was already inscribed in the constitution. Both issues provoked major controversy in Ireland. What was Sinn Fein's position?

Given its longstanding policy of condemning abortion, Sinn Fein did not participate in the 1983 debate. While many of its more radical supporters were active in the campaign against the amendment, the republican movement itself remained aloof. Even the more radical republicans, however, did not campaign in support of the right to abortion—they followed the mainstream radical line of avoiding the issue of abortion and opposing the constitutional amendment on diverse technical and libertarian grounds.

The 1983 controversy did produce some change in Sinn Fein policy. At the Ard Fheis that year, the policy statement that 'We are totally opposed to abortion' was amended by removing the word 'totally'. In 1985 the growth of feminist influence in Sinn Fein resulted in the Ard Fheis approving, at an ill-attended session, a clause appending support for 'a woman's right to choose' to the existing anti-abortion policy. The republican movement was trying to have it both ways. However, in the run-up to the 1986 Ard Fheis, with the prospect of an imminent general election in the Free State, the republican press was flooded with demands to drop the right to choose clause.

On the one hand, dogmatic Catholics insisted on the absolute rights of the unborn child. On the other hand, liberals struggled to make out that upholding the right to choose did not indicate approval for abortion. But for women in Ireland, abortion is not a matter of choice, but a question of the rights of women to participate in society by limiting their role as child-bearers. The vacillation of the liberals made certain the victory of the dogmatists—a victory abetted by those who put Sinn Fein's fears of losing Catholic votes above its commitment to women's rights. Sinn Fein ended up with a policy on abortion which was more right-wing not only than the British Conservative Party, but than most of the mainstream Irish parties too.

When the abortion issue flared up again in 1992, Sinn Fein again squirmed around it, heroically upholding 'a woman's right to travel or receive information' and even demanding that 'non-directive pregnancy counselling embodying all choices should be freely available' (*AP/RN*, 19 November 1992). In a society where abortion is illegal, there is clearly no choice and little point in counselling. Sinn Fein also vehemently denounced 'the attitudes and forces in society that compel women to have abortions', while insisting that 'we accept the need for abortion only where a woman's life is at risk or in grave danger (eg, all forms of cancer)' (*AP/RN*, 5 March 1992).

An attempt to reverse the anti-abortion policy was defeated at the

1993 Ard Fheis, after senior figures including Adams, Hartley and Gibney spoke against it. Gibney explained that the existing policy was 'a good compromise between the conservative forces in society and the women's position' (*AP/RN*, 25 February 1993). The result of what one of Sinn Fein's key election organisers regards as a 'good compromise' is that Sinn Fein has been left trailing behind secularising trends in Irish society which have been led by the virulently anti-republican middle classes.

The divorce referendum in 1986 was another test of Sinn Fein's commitment to women's rights. On divorce public prejudice was less intense than on the issue of abortion, so the republican movement could venture a bolder line. It openly supported the demand for more liberal legislation on divorce and called for a 'Yes' vote for constitutional reform. However, instead of insisting on the importance of fighting for the further extension of women's rights, *AP/RN* reassured its readers that 'the divorce referendum represents no threat to marriage or the family in the Twenty-Six Counties' (19 June 1986). For Sinn Fein, again, it was a matter of conscience and choice, not women's rights. Instead of combating the influence of Catholic reaction on its supporters, Sinn Fein bent over backwards to indulge them. Sinn Fein's weasel words about divorce did nothing to undermine a climate of opinion which ensured a massive 'No' in the referendum.

The election results in the South confirm that Sinn Fein's curious synthesis of traditional republicanism, old-style state socialism and Catholic pietism has little popular appeal, especially among the young people who are Ireland's future. The irrelevance of Sinn Fein's programme is disguised in the North, where a vote for Sinn Fein is more an expression of approval for the IRA than the outcome of detailed scrutiny of the party's plans for 'democratic structures in a free Ireland'. Yet if the republican movement proceeds down the road prepared by its 'peace process' and Sinn Fein can no longer benefit from its association with the armed struggle, the party before long will have to justify itself with its own policies. The decision by the Dublin government in January 1994 to abandon its draconian censorship of republicans from the broadcast media is a welcome removal of a restriction on democratic rights. But it is one which deprives Sinn Fein of its main excuse for electoral failure, leaving it with no more alibis.

When the Hume-Adams dialogue became public in 1993, many commentators feared that respectable Catholic nationalism would be compromised and that the SDLP might lose support to Sinn Fein. Yet once Hume has achieved his mission of integrating the republican movement into some British-imposed settlement, then Adams risks becoming just another constitutional nationalist politician, and Sinn Fein merely a radical appendage of the SDLP.

4

The South: a quest for identity

> In the event of an overall settlement, the Irish government will, as part of a balanced constitutional accommodation, put forward and support proposals for change in the Irish constitution which would fully reflect the principle of consent in Northern Ireland. ('Joint Declaration', December 1993)

Dramatic changes have swept the Irish Republic in recent years. Old traditions and political institutions which seemed such an intrinsic part of the Republic's make-up for generations have, in the course of a few years, faded from view or been discredited in the eyes of the public. Ideas which would once have been considered heretical have become common sense. The Downing Street declaration articulated the scale of the change in the commitment on the part of the Dublin government to alter the constitution of the state and abandon the claim over the North of Ireland.

Ireland, for so long the bastion of sacred ritual, both public and private, seems almost overnight to have turned into its opposite. Nothing appears to be sacred in Ireland any more. Traditional nationalism with its commitment to a united Ireland is dead, the Catholic church has shrunk from public life and is no longer the object of popular veneration. Once renowned throughout Europe for its sexual repression and taboos, in June 1993 the Republic set the age of consent for homosexuals at 17 years of age while it was still 21 in Britain.

Southern politicians and commentators speak with pride of the transition from old-style Catholic nationalism to a modern European state:

The days of the sexually frustrated bachelors and old maids, the days of de Valera's happy maidens and frugal comforts, are well gone. Sex, which was surrounded by fear and ignorance, is no longer the bogey that it was. Self-esteem has been restored after decades of repression imposed, since 1922, not by a foreign power but from within. Ireland stands on the threshold of a new era when its potential may be fully realized. (G Hussey, *Ireland Today: Anatomy of a Changing Nation*, 1993, p4)

There can be no doubting the scale of the changes taking place in Ireland today. But is it modernising in the sense that it is becoming a democratic, secular state? There is a fundamental flaw in assuming that the destruction of the old political system necessarily means Ireland is moving into the mainstream of European politics. The problem with using a model of development such as modernisation is that the specific features of Irish politics and society are obscured. Closer examination of what is happening in the Republic suggests that it is evolving not towards democracy and secularism, but into something quite new for which the labels of conventional political analysis prove inadequate. Let's first look at what has changed, particularly at the level of politics. We will then examine the factors which have held the Republic aloof from European politics for so long. Finally, we will assess the political forces which are shaping the new Ireland and the prospects for change in the future.

Nationalism in retreat

The diminishing appeal of Irish nationalism—at least to the political class—is shown in the response of all the main parties to the commemoration of the Easter Rising of 1916, the key date in the nationalist calendar. The fiftieth anniversary of the Rising in 1966 was marked by a week of celebrations, television documentaries and countless newspaper articles and books. De Valera, himself a veteran of the Rising, spoke in front of the General Post Office, where 50 years earlier the Proclamation of Independence had been read, reminding those present of the importance of reclaiming the North. No dissenting voice was permitted. One Jesuit priest who submitted an article to an academic journal criticising the leader of the Rising, Patrick Pearse, was told bluntly that his article was unsuitable for publication.

In 1991 the government commemorated the seventy-fifth anniversary of the Rising. This time the dignitaries at the GPO could not hide their discomfort at the proceedings. Albert Reynolds and president Mary Robinson addressed a small gathering, this time talking about the need for reconciliation and respect for diverse traditions. There was no avoiding the fact that the language of reconciliation and diversity would have been anathema to the leaders of the Rising. Both Patrick Pearse and James Connolly, the two leading signatories of the proclamation of 1916, were violently opposed to partition, and Connolly in particular held Unionism and its apologists in contempt.

The embarrassed response to 1916 shows the difficulties involved in severing the link with the past. On the one hand, Irish politicians feel that their status as a modern nation is enhanced by ditching nationalist tradition. On the other, those traditions have become integral to the state's authority and identity. Since 1922 the Easter Rising has been successfully incorporated into the genealogy of the state. Indeed, it was reinterpreted by subsequent Irish governments as the moment of the state's conception. Bringing such a crucial event into disrepute eats away at the moral fabric of the state itself. Two prominent historians, Mairin Ni Dhonnchadha and Theo Dorgan, expressed unease at the authorities' wish to forget the embarrassment of Easter 1916: 'There are those of us who feel that, as a reaction, amnesia—private or communal—is both unhealthy and dangerous.' (M Ni Dhonnchadha and T Dorgan (eds), *Revising the Rising*, 1991, pix)

Notwithstanding these historians' anxieties, the predominant interpretation of 1916 in 1991 was along the lines proposed by Fintan O'Toole, writing in the *Irish Times* on the seventy-fifth anniversary of the Rising. O'Toole suggested that the culmination of the project of nationhood initiated by Pearse, Connolly and the other leaders of 1916 was Ireland's status as a European country recognised as a member of the European Community: '1991 is not just the seventy-fifth anniversary of the Rising, it is also the year before 1992....They may not have known it but what the men and women of 1916 fought for was an Irish seat at the European table. The Rising began with a European conflict

and may well end, at long last, with a European integration.'
('They fought for a seat at the European table', 30 March 1991)

The embarrassment felt by the political establishment at the commemoration of Easter 1916 has come under attack from the proponents of the theory of post-colonialism. According to this doctrine the
colonial legacy has left a deep imprint on the Irish mind, causing a ser-
vility towards the dominant power and a denigrating attitude towards
anything native. According to one post-colonial writer:

> The problem with many nationalisms is that they leave the hege-
> mony of the original imperialist categories of thought unchallenged;
> and unchallenged too is the imperialist conceit that the natives are in
> all respects the polar opposites of their masters. (D Kiberd, *Irish
> Reporter*, No6, 1992)

The theory of post-colonialism relegates Britain's political influence
to the past and dwells on the psychological and cultural residues of
colonialism. Later in this chapter we will look more closely at how
the question of culture has come to dominate Irish politics. The theory
of post-colonialism is closely related to notions of an Irish cultural
identity. It is a highly plastic and apologetic doctrine.

The theory of post-colonialism can recognise the enduring backwardness and distortions of Irish society, while exonerating Britain of
any blame for their continuation. It also panders to a residual nationalism by celebrating all things Irish. It can incorporate elements of the
republican critique of imperial authority, while at the same time
demonstrating its irrelevance today. Like most 'post-' words, it is an
attempt to transcend in rhetoric what has not been transcended in substance. (For a good example of the post-colonialism thesis, see JJ Lee,
Ireland 1912-85: Government and Society, 1988.)

Whatever else it may be, the South of Ireland is not a post-colonial
society. Unlike Algeria or Vietnam, the Irish state was not born out of
a successful movement for national independence. Even a comparison
with a country like Kenya is excessively generous. Although the British
smashed the Kenyan Mau Mau revolt in the 1950s, it did subsequently
withdraw and grant Kenyan independence. Not only was the Irish state
born out of the defeat of the liberation movement, but Britain

reinforced its presence in the North of Ireland under the partition set-tlement. The failure of the struggle for national independence from 1916 to 1923 left the South of Ireland weak and incapable of mapping out any independent destiny for itself.

The project of creating a post-colonial Ireland has fixed upon the symbolic importance of articles 2 and 3 of the Irish constitution, that lay claim to the North of Ireland. Articles 2 and 3 have been identified both by Loyalists in the North and the champions of post-colonialism in the South as a barrier to the normalisation of relations between Ireland and the United Kingdom.

The meaning of the constitution

Articles 2 and 3 of the Irish constitution declare the national territory to be all 32 counties of Ireland, and claim jurisdiction over the entire country, not just the 26 counties of the Republic. They implicitly com-mit every Irish government, irrespective of party, to work towards the goal of Irish unity. The Unionists have adduced them as evidence of irredentism and proof that the Republic is not to be trusted. The British, more sanguine about the importance of constitutional dress-ing, have used them as a way of putting pressure on Dublin to make greater concessions on security.

The logic of Articles 2 and 3 is rooted in the nature of the Irish Republic. As a compromised entity pulled together out of those parts of Ireland left over by the British, the Southern state is lumbered with a problem of legitimacy. Nobody in Ireland ever fought for a 26-county state, and on its own it has no reason to exist as an independent entity. This problem was recognised from the very beginning by Michael Collins, the former IRA leader and chief Irish signatory to the Treaty of 1921. He described the Treaty as a 'stepping stone' to full inde-pendence, 'the freedom to achieve freedom'. In other words, the state itself was only legitimate as part of the process of achieving full independence.

This formula was later codified into the Irish constitution by Eamon de Valera, Collins' enemy in the Civil War which followed the signing of the Treaty. Articles 2 and 3 of the 1937 constitution are the political foundation of the Southern state. It is these two articles which bridge the gap between the reality of an artificially imposed regime and the aspiration for a unitary, independent nation state. The articles acknowledge the transitory character of the existing arrangement, and establish the state as a stage on the road to Irish unity.

In reality, few Southern politicians ever had the slightest intention of enforcing the constitution. The claim over the Six Counties is a way of linking the South to the legacy of national resistance to British rule, a legacy which commanded great respect among the bulk of the population. By linking the institutions of the Twenty-Six Counties with the whole tradition of nationalism, and especially its most recent expressions, the 1916 Rising and the Tan War of 1919-21, the leaders of the South could claim to be the legitimate heirs of that tradition and the agents of its consummation.

Articles 2 and 3 can be compared with Clause Four of the British Labour Party, which commits the party to socialism. Like articles 2 and 3, Clause Four has no practical consequences. Successive Labour governments ran British capitalism in much the same way as the Conservatives. But it was Clause Four which gave the party its identity. Although Clause Four is still in place, the commitment to state socialism associated with it has been abandoned. Without that commitment the Labour Party has been left rudderless and prone to question its very existence. It is notable that the Labour spokesman on Northern Ireland, Kevin McNamara, in a speech in Cork in October 1993, warned of the dangers of hasty constitutional changes. McNamara has direct experience of the consequences of ditching an identity intrinsic to the make-up of a political institution.

The abandonment of articles 2 and 3 could cause serious trouble for the Republic. The rhetorical challenge to partition posed by the articles established a link between the Southern government and the aspirations of Irish nationalism. At the same time, they had the effect of removing the national question from public debate. The constitutional claim to the North postponed the achievement of national unity into the indefinite future and left the governing classes to get on with the day-to-day running of their new state. In such an artificial state, the use of artificial devices built into the constitution is a prerequisite for political stability.

To understand the dangers for the ruling classes in the South in turning away from the past, it is necessary to see just how dependent Irish society has been upon tradition for its stability to date. The Twenty-Six Counties' putative status as a post-colonial society throws into light the two central tenets of tradition: nationalism and Catholicism. Let's look at each in turn.

Looking to the past—nationalism

Nationalism was a great source of stability for the South. It endowed the state with an historic legitimacy which it would otherwise have lacked. Considering the economic backwardness and social stagnation that have characterised the state since its inception, the level of social peace is remarkable. There is a deep sense of loyalty among Irish people to the Twenty-Six Counties which could never have been created and sustained without that identification with the old struggle for independence.

The nationalism of the Republic is a distinctive blend of liberationary aspirations and reactionary institutions. By bringing together republican rhetoric, Catholicism, revival of the Irish language and promotion of native culture, the Southern regime created a recognisable identity for itself.

One face of the identity is the so-called 'Green card', played by Southern politicians, particularly in the dominant Fianna Fail Party. The Green card is primarily a way of dissipating nationalist sentiment through its controlled expression. It was first used in the 1930s by Eamon de Valera when he revoked the Oath of Allegiance to the King which had until then been the most divisive clause in the Treaty of 1921. During the Second World War he successfully tapped nationalist sentiment by keeping the Free State neutral, even though in secret he allowed British aircraft to use Irish airspace and territory.

His successors in Fianna Fail were no less adept at manipulating nationalism. When the pogroms in the North broke out in 1969, the then Taoiseach, Jack Lynch, declared 'we will not stand idly by' and deployed troops along the Border. In the event not only did he stand idly by, but he clamped down on all IRA activities. But the rhetoric was enough to assuage Southern fears. His successor, Charles Haughey, was a master player of the Green card, matched only by de Valera.

He landed himself in court in 1970 in the famous 'Arms trial', in which he and two other government ministers were implicated in an attempt to smuggle arms to the IRA. Haughey was acquitted but secured his reputation in the heart of nationalist Ireland.

Because of the diminishing nationalist sentiment in the South, the pressure to play the Green card has also diminished over the years. Only when the struggle in the North became particularly intense or when Britain openly offended Irish sensibilities did national sentiment agitate public opinion. In 1972, following Bloody Sunday in Derry when British paratroopers shot dead 14 unarmed demonstrators, the Dublin government sent a letter of protest and made little effort to stop a crowd in Dublin burning down the British embassy. Following the release of the Guildford Four in 1989, Haughey met those released and wept before the television cameras.

There was always a great disparity between the rhetoric and reality of Southern nationalism. Governments in the Republic crack down hard on republicans who try to give substance to the rhetoric of nationalism and unite the divided country. As soon as the state was founded it acquired a reputation for repression which made even the old British administration look benign. Former republicans such as Eamon de Valera had no qualms about interning and hanging IRA members— even to the extent of borrowing Britain's hangman Albert Pierpoint to do the job. An Offences against the State Act exists which allows the authorities to jail anyone whom a Garda (police) officer suspects of IRA membership.

In 1973 the Republic introduced a broadcasting ban, Section 31, forbidding interviews with republican representatives. This ban was much more thorough than that introduced in 1988 by the British government. In Britain it was only the direct transmission of the voices of republicans that was prohibited, whereas in the South, the substance of interviews were banned from the airwaves. In January 1994 the ban was lifted as an enticement to Sinn Fein to accept the Joint Declaration. However as the minister responsible, Michael D Higgins, made clear, Section 18 of the Broadcasting Act of 1960 could serve just as well to keep off the airwaves anything to which the government objected.

The Southern regime used other means to define a new identity for itself. The Irish language and Irish culture were systematically cultivated from the foundation of the state. From the eighteenth century, Irish had been slowly eradicated through suppression and the encroachment of a superior culture. In the nineteenth century the use of Irish was considered irrelevant by the nationalist movement. Neither the Fenians nor Charles Stewart Parnell, the leader of the Irish Home Rule Party at Westminster, gave it much thought. English was the *lingua franca* of both political and everyday life.

The Gaelic Revival of the 1890s, led by Douglas Hyde (later to become the first president of the Free State), made the Gaelicisation of Ireland the central plank of its policy. In common with nationalist movements in other parts of Europe, the revival of the language reflected a disenchantment with the dynamic of modern life and a desire to retreat into a romanticised past. Ironically revivalism was at the outset a movement of the Anglo-Irish aristocracy anxious to define a role for itself in a world increasingly at odds with its own values. However, it was subsequently hijacked by the middle class nationalist movement which sprang up in the years before the First World War.

The new state formed in 1922 made great play of its regard for the language. The government imposed Irish language lessons in the schools and made qualification in Irish compulsory for those entering the civil service. Even though the language was redundant as a means of communication, its imposition was useful for the state in building up its reputation as a defender of Irish identity.

Since the outbreak of the war in the North in 1969, the attraction of nationalism in the South, especially to the political class, has faded considerably. Once the conflict began, the nationalist rhetoric could not be so neatly disentangled from the threat posed by the IRA. Southern politicians were highly sensitive to charges from British and Unionist politicians that they gave succour to the IRA through their irredentist claim over the North and their anti-British rhetoric.

Nationalism and Catholicism were the two defining features of the Republic. For over 60 years the Catholic church held Ireland in a moral stranglehold. The Irish middle classes lacked the coherence and strength to create a genuinely new order out of the state allocated to them by Britain. Instead they looked to religion to help to provide a sense of identity.

Looking to the past—Catholicism

Irish Catholicism is often presented as a faith with deep roots in the national psyche. One of the benefits of the recent changes in Ireland is that the declining support for the church makes that analysis untenable. In fact, Irish Catholicism is peculiar in the degree to which it was constructed and moulded around the needs of political power; hence its highly coercive character. The failure to understand the complex dynamic between the temporal and spiritual powers in Ireland has led many writers on the subject to elevate the church into an autonomous power.

For most of the eighteenth century Catholicism was suppressed by the British government and Protestantism promoted under the infamous penal laws. However, by the time of the Act of Union, sections of the British establishment were moving towards an accommodation with the church. The Catholic conservative thinker Edmund Burke was a strong supporter of Catholic emancipation. He recommended a closer alliance between the government and the church to ensure stability in Ireland and prevent the spread of the ideas of the French Revolution.

In 1845 the Catholic orator Richard Lalor Shiel told the House of Commons of the benefits it would gain from funding the Catholic college for priests at Maynooth:

> You must not take the Catholic clergy into your pay, but you can take the Catholic clergy under your care....Are not lectures at Maynooth cheaper than state prosecutions? Are not professors less costly than Crown solicitors? Is not a large standing army and a great constabulary force more expensive than the moral police with which by the priesthood of Ireland you can be thriftily and efficaciously supplied? (Quoted in J Connolly, *Labour, Nationality and Religion*, 1969, p15)

The government took Lalor Shiel's advice and funded the college at Maynooth. In 1869 the Church of Ireland was disestablished and in the 1870s Cardinal Henry Newman arrived from Oxford to found the Catholic university in Dublin.

The church made its most forceful entry into politics in the campaign against Fenianism in the 1860s. The hierarchy attacked militant nationalism, the Bishop of Kerry declaring that 'hell was not hot enough nor eternity long enough to punish such miscreants'. During the Tan War of 1919-21, and more especially in the Civil War which followed, the Catholic hierarchy denounced the liberation movement. Since 1969 the same implacable hostility has been displayed in the church's attacks on the IRA.

However, the church's orientation to physical-force republicanism was never entirely one-dimensional and hostile. Even if the hierarchy has remained consistent in its condemnations of the IRA, the ordinary clergy have always been more ambivalent, especially when placed in situations of intense conflict between the colonial authorities and the people, in the past throughout Ireland and in the North to this day. Faced with the everyday consequences of British domination, the parish priest is forced to adjust and at least tone down the outbursts of his superiors. Clergy who have followed the political line of the hierarchy have been ostracised by their parishioners while those showing more sympathy have secured continuing loyalty to the church. The division of labour between hierarchy and clergy gave the church as a whole the flexibility to manoeuvre between the two hostile camps.

The church had the added advantage of being able to accommodate to the new nationalism which developed in the Twenty-Six Counties following the Treaty. The failure to achieve full independence brought into play the more backward aspects of the nationalist tradition. The nationalism of the Free State was inward-looking and parochial. Religion became central to the Irish state not only as a means of social control, but also as a symbol of independence from Protestant England.

The alliance between the new nationalism identified with the 26-county state and Catholicism invested the church with political legitimacy. The church established some political distance from London at the end of the nineteenth century. The ultramontane movement within the Catholic church was initiated by the First Vatican Council of 1870. It stressed the precedence of spiritual over temporal power, reinforced the centrality of Rome as the seat of all spiritual power, and propounded the doctrine of papal infallibility. Ultramontanism in general was a response to the threat posed by new European nationalist movements such as the anti-clerical Risorgimento in Italy. The Irish church became strongly ultramontanist due to its ambivalent relations with the Protestant authorities.

The growing importance of the Roman connection provided the church with a useful source of moral authority. Rome became a focus of power within Ireland, giving the Irish people an alternative political orbit and distancing the church from the close bond that it had formed with London.

The new alliance between church and state in Ireland was celebrated at the Eucharistic Congress of 1932, when hundreds of thousands of Irish people made their way to the Phoenix Park near Dublin to hear the papal legate celebrate high mass. Not only was it a religious ceremony, it was also a celebration of nationalist Ireland and the endurance of Catholicism and the national spirit through hundreds of years of British domination. De Valera's St Patrick's day broadcast in 1935 drew the connection between Catholicism and nationalism:

> Ireland remains a Catholic nation, and as such sets the eternal destiny of man high above the isms and idols of the day. The State will be confined to its functions as guardian of the rights of the individual and the family, coordinator of the activities of its citizens. (Quoted in *Ireland Today*, p157)

The most distinctive thing about Irish Catholicism, however, is not so much its political posture as the way in which it has invaded the sphere of private life. In this it is quite distinct from Catholicism elsewhere. Italian Catholicism, for example, strongly identifies with the established power and publicly opposes abortion and divorce. But in practice it takes a more worldly attitude in attempting to impose its strictures, knowing the gulf there is between what people say in public and do in private. In Ireland, however, the church from the middle of the nineteenth century embarked on a full-scale invasion of private life.

The utility of moral control in such a troublesome colony was not lost on the imperial authorities. From the end of the nineteenth century the state began to finance religious schooling, new religious orders, and the establishment of new parishes. The cult of the Blessed Virgin Mary, with all its overtones of sexual abstinence, was actively promoted. The church took to policing the most intimate details of people's lives, embarking on one of the most remarkable campaigns of moral engineering ever attempted. The family was the central institution through which this policy was enforced. In rural areas especially, the insecurity generated by the struggle for land made conformity to family values a matter of economic survival.

After 1921 the rulers of the new state, faced with a disaffected and sullen populace, reinforced the system of moral control, insitutionalising support for church and family and integrating the church into the nationalist identity. The 1937 constitution defined women's role within the family (Article 41) and enshrined the special position of the Catholic church in the new state (Article 44, dropped in 1972). Moral conformity, with all the guilt and abstinence associated with it, became the norm in Ireland.

The state's alliance with the Catholic church reflected its inability to break from the past and its reliance on moral coercion to maintain stability. The Irish people, and women in particular, paid a terrible price for the moral straitjacket imposed by church and state. Divorce, contraception and abortion were all forbidden. Every year thousands of Irish women travel to Britain to seek abortions. In 1983, a referendum resulted in abortion becoming a constitutional offence. This made it possible for the police to prosecute any woman travelling to England for an abortion.

Like nationalism, Catholicism had become a mainstay of the Irish state created in the 26 counties of Southern Ireland by the Treaty of 1921. But in more recent years, the dissolution of the politics of the Civil War has called into question both of these elements of the Southern Irish national identity.

The end of Civil War politics

When Mary Robinson was elected president in 1990, the event was hailed both in Ireland and abroad as an end to the Civil War politics which had dominated the state since its foundation. For most of its history, the Republic was considered a country where both politics and social attitudes were frozen in the 1920s. The command which the Catholic church had over the moral life of Irish people and the general backwardness of society reinforced the prevailing prejudices. All the major Irish parties reflect the Republic's preoccupation with past traditions. Fine Gael and Fianna Fail are still identified by the part they played in the Civil War.

Fine Gael, which emerged out of the pro-Treaty forces of the early days of the Free State, has traditionally been associated with big farmers and the middle classes, and with pro-British policies. For this reason, its electoral support has always been limited, proving unable to mobilise enough popular support to form a majority government. All its brief spells in office have been in unstable coalitions—usually with the Labour Party. The last time it held government was in the period from 1983 to 1987, when it was crushed at the polls.

Fianna Fail, which lays claim to the republican tradition of those who fought against the Treaty in 1922, has looked to the working class and to small farmers, especially in the west. It is weak in Dublin's middle class suburbs. Traditionally it maintained a strong base of support through a mixture of anti-British rhetoric and political patronage. Through the use of these twin tactics, Fianna Fail established deep roots in Irish society.

Demographic changes and the waning of nationalism have undermined Fianna Fail's traditional support. In urban Dublin, the old nationalist rhetoric holds less sway and patronage can not be conducted with the same ease as in a rural community. In the 1980s Charles Haughey offset the diminishing fortunes of his party through shrewd political manoeuvring. Without any obvious alternative to Fianna Fail, Haughey hung on to power, though his administration was beset by scandal and defections. The regime of 'the Boss' became a byword for the patrician sleaze of Ireland's Civil War parties. Haughey's successor, Albert Reynolds, is a shadow of the Boss.

The fate of Fianna Fail is indicative of the fate of nationalism as such in Southern Ireland. The rise of Irish nationalism coincides with the rise of nationalisms throughout the third world. First came the anti-colonial movements of the interwar period and after the war many new nations—the 26-county republic among them—set about building independent countries. First under de Valera and later under Sean Lemass, the Twenty-Six Counties echoed the developing world's strategy of building up local industry while trying to shut foreign consumer goods out.

The South's autarkic economic development, like that of much of the third world, did not allow it to catch up with the developed West. But the failure of separate development was not restricted to the sphere of economics. The outbreak of war in the North indicated the limits of national sentiment in the South.

When military conflict erupted in the North between a rejuvenated republican movement and the British state, nationalism in the South became a more tendentious proposition. It was one thing to wage rhetorically an economic war with the British in the thirties. It was quite another to wage a shooting war with the British in the seventies. In the event, the Republic's ruling elite preferred to cooperate with the British policy of containing the armed struggle, rather than risk out-right conflict with so powerful a neighbour. The Dublin government had good reason to fear the consequences of a renewed struggle for national liberation upon the institutions of the 26-county Republic.

Until 1969 nationalism had served both as an organising principle for Irish society and as a way of relating to the rest of the world. But once war broke out, nationalism became a barrier to Ireland's relations with the West and a source of instability at home. The project of build-ing an independent nation had turned from being a boon to a bur-den—robbing Fianna Fail of its central political goal. All that was left was the trappings of power, the patronage that without the national principle to hold it in place looked more and more like old-fashioned corruption. Fianna Fail's electoral decline has been slow if steady. At its peak in 1977, the party had 51 per cent of the total poll. At the last elec-tion in 1992, it received just 38 per cent.

Founded in 1917, the Labour Party is the oldest constitutional party in Ireland, and until recently, the least relevant. Despite its name it was never really a working class party. Its links with the unions were always tenuous—they invested more effort in forging links with Fianna Fail—and in 1992 the Labour Party was funded by the unions to the tune of just IR£25 000. Labour's political fortunes rose dramatically follow-ing the general election of November 1992. To examine Labour's role in the election we need to look at the broader shifts which took place in Irish politics.

The first thing to notice about the changes in Irish politics is how slow they've been, and to what a limited extent social changes have registered in the political system. All the same parties that were there 50 years ago are still in place, and those which have attempted to 'break the mould of Irish politics' have generally achieved little. The Progressive Democrats, formed in 1985, promised a start to a more normal left/right politics. After winning 13 per cent of the vote in the 1987 election, they subsequently embarked on a steady decline to the point where they now have only four TDs in parliament. Civil War politics persisted right up until the 1990s.

The other noticeable feature of the recent successes of parties and individuals who claim to lie outside the Civil War divide is the fortuitous character of their victories. The best example of that is the election of Mary Robinson as president in November 1990.

The presidential contest started out as a three-way contest between Robinson, Fianna Fail candidate Brian Lenihan and Fine Gael candidate Austin Currie. Originally Robinson was in third place, but after hard campaigning she managed to overtake the lacklustre Currie. Both were still a long way behind Lenihan. The turning point came when Lenihan denied allegations of attempting to interfere with the constitutional decisions of the previous presidential incumbent, Patrick Hillery. Everybody knew that Lenihan had attempted to interfere with Hillery's decisions since he had admitted as much on a previous occasion. His bare-faced denials of the truth only aggravated the situation and created a sense of disgust among the electorate at the dishonesty of Fianna Fail. Robinson won the election, not because of a great swell of support for what she stood for, but because of the backlash against Fianna Fail.

The same pattern was evident in the 1992 election when the Labour Party for the first time in its history made an electoral breakthrough, doubling its Dail representation from 16 to 33 TDs. The 1992 Labour Party was little different from the old Labour Party. It lacked any base of support in the country and could only afford to stand candidates in a minority of constituencies. The success of the Labour Party led by Dick Spring was due to the decline of the old parties, both Fianna Fail and Fine Gael. Spring was like the Ross Perot of Irish politics, he happened to be in the right place at the right time, when the disenchantment with all his rivals was at its most intense.

Much of the impetus for change corresponded to a shift which took place within the Southern Irish establishment itself. Traditionally, the leading social groups within the political parties were based in the countryside. The demographic shift from country to town which began in the 1960s slowly changed the composition of the political elite. By the 1980s a more urban middle class, with less regard for the Catholic church than the rural middle class, had taken control in Dublin.

Until the late eighties this group was too weak and supine to challenge the traditional structures. International developments, and a mood for change, though incoherently expressed, prompted this group to air its views more openly. The election of Mary Robinson as president in 1990 followed by the electoral advance of the Irish Labour Party in 1992 marks the end of the old nationalist era and the beginning of the pluralist one.

The real force behind the changes in Irish politics has proved to be not so much the force of the new as the decay of the old. As the old parties left by the Civil War have fallen into disrepute, others have had their chance. The extent to which the changes in Irish politics have been governed by the weakening of the old institutions is also true of the apparent shifts in morality. Here too the appearance of new mores and attitudes is more indicative of the declining authority of the Catholic church.

The tightened strictures on abortion coming out of the 1983 referendum proved to be a Pyrrhic victory for the church, only illustrating the difficulties in reconciling an inflexible moral code with a young, urban working class population.

In February 1992 the 'X' case rocked Ireland. 'X' was a 14-year old girl who, after becoming pregnant as a result of rape, was forbidden by the high court from leaving Ireland for an abortion. The spectacle of elderly politicians and churchmen restraining the girl from travelling abroad for an abortion appalled people throughout the South. The extremity of the case forced the government to come up with a new round of amendments which would remove the restrictions on travel and information, and allow for abortion in circumstances where the life of the woman was threatened. The right to travel and information—euphemisms for the right to an abortion in Britain—was supported in a referendum, though even the limited access to abortion in the Twenty-Six Counties proposed by the referendum was rejected.

Nonetheless, in 1992 the supreme court, reluctant to be left policing dangerous pregnancies, allowed abortion where a grave risk to the life of the woman exists.

There has been a significant, if slow, shift within sections of the population on moral questions in recent years. The weakening of religion has both political and social causes. At a social level it is a simple fact that Catholicism operates most effectively in a rural society where the job of moral policing can be carried out with some degree of success. Once Southern Ireland started to change from being a rural to an urban society, then the influence of religion inevitably weakened. In 1926, over half the population worked in agriculture. By the late eighties, that figure had dropped to 12 per cent. From the sixties, the move to the cities accelerated with the creation of large working class estates around Dublin and other cities.

With urbanisation came the loosening of the traditional ties of church and family. Irish cities were little different from the cities of any other modern society, with the opportunities and social problems associated with them. Many of the old prohibitions became increasingly anachronistic. What was the point in banning divorce when single-parent families were becoming more common in many parts of Dublin? And didn't banning contraception only make a laughing-stock of the government when young people were pursuing their pleasure like everybody else around the world? From the late sixties the old prohibitions became increasingly unpopular throughout Irish society. The shifting social patterns are reflected in the level of church attendance. Across the country as a whole, 80 per cent of people go to Sunday mass. However in new working class areas on the outskirts of the city, the figure is as low as five per cent.

It is impossible for the church to operate in the old way. Moral absolutes are no longer acceptable in the pluralist society which Ireland has become. In the old days the church threatened eternal damnation for those who disobeyed its rules, especially its rules concerning sex. Such a policy worked in a society where the doctrines of the church were widely accepted. Now that moral guidelines have become less precise, the church has responded by trying to replace moral absolutes with social arguments. Through the eighties the church leaned more and more on social arguments against abortion, divorce and contraception, suggesting that these facilities would lead to greater economic insecurity for women.

The other factor threatening the church is the general disrepute into which the institutions identified with the old order have fallen. The national church is diminished with the loss of the legitimacy conferred by the state. As it becomes more acceptable to criticise the church's shortcomings, the sort of scandals that would have been brushed under the carpet before are fully publicised. In May 1992 Bishop Eamonn Casey resigned following the revelation that he had fathered a child in 1973, and subsequently spurned both mother and child. The scandal shocked Ireland and led to a sharp fall in donations to the church. Without doubt, we can look forward to even greater and more lurid scandals in the future.

Where the state and Catholicism coalesced in the 26-county Republic forged by de Valera and ruled largely by his Fianna Fail party, these two forces are no longer holding each other up. The Southern Ireland of the fifties was a profoundly foreign country to any European visitor. The combination of Civil War politics and a traditionalist Irish church embodied that sense of isolation. Today the South is much more influenced by the culture and mores of Britain and the rest of Europe. Television and other mass media contribute to a sense of a European state rather than a developing country. The church's ability to limit the availability of sexually explicit material or information about abortion or depictions of homosexuality is constrained by the impact of a European mass culture.

As people's hopes turn towards Europe as an avenue for Irish national sentiment, the institutional influence of the Catholic church looks more and more like a barrier to modernisation. The recent legalisation of homosexuality indicated the extent to which the church takes second place to the need to bring Irish law into line with the European Convention on Human Rights.

Even though pluralism and scandal eat away at the church's moral authority, it would be wrong to imagine that Ireland is becoming a secular society. It is striking how little anti-clerical sentiment there is within the middle classes which run the state. They still have as cosy a relationship with the church as they ever had. In fact the clergy themselves have played a prominent part in the creation of the new pluralist society. Despite the dwindling numbers of the faithful, the church still runs the educational system, its views are canvassed on radio and television on every conceivable issue. In working class areas, state-funded community groups organised through the churches provide a link between the state and this section of society. In effect, a trade-off has taken place between church and state. In return for the church toning down its moral prohibitions (which it could not enforce anyway), the state has allowed the church to maintain its grip on the institutions and a privileged position in society. Church and state are still united. But both have changed. Defining Ireland as modern given these factors can only imply a radical redefinition of the meaning of modernity.

The decline of the old parties of Civil War politics, and the new role of the church, raises the question of what is to replace the old order. None of the old parties and institutions represent the new values of Irish society. To be more precise, they don't have any values. Reynolds' rhetoric about a 'pragmatic' new Fianna Fail shows how even the strongest party in the Twenty-Six Counties has lost its direction. The end of nationalist ideology has left the old parties without a sense of direction. There really is no difference now between the two main parties, both are without form or character, like their leaders. Labour may be able to take advantage of their decline momentarily, but it will soon confront the same problem: what does it stand for?

We now need to examine the value system that has emerged in the Republic in recent years as a response to the decline of nationalism. Understanding the idea of pluralism in Irish politics and culture gives us some clues as to the shape of things to come.

From nationalism to pluralism

The idea of pluralism is that no one culture is superior to another. All cultures should be cherished equally as part of the diverse tapestry which makes up society. The word was coined by an Englishman, Arthur Bentley, but the concept as we know it today was developed in America by Horace Kallen in a series of lectures reproduced in his book *Cultural Pluralism and the American Idea: An Essay in Social Philosophy* (1956).

Pluralism in Ireland, however, means something rather different.

In America, Horace Kallen was writing about the negotiation between a variety of ethnic groups over influence in the state. In Ireland, there is not strictly speaking a plurality, but a duality—between Britain and Ireland. Relocated from politics into populations, the duality is one between nationalists and Unionists. Further translated into culture, the duality is between the nationalist tradition and the Unionist tradition—the terms in which the current discussion is held.

The transition from nationalism to pluralism revolves around the two traditions and the extent to which they can be reconciled. In the first instance this transition is one that reconciles traditional Irish nationalism to the perpetuation of Britain's influence in the North, by granting legitimacy to the claims of the Unionist minority in the island. As we shall see the matter does not rest there, but tends towards a redefinition of Irish national identity in favour of a cultural identity, excised of its popular dimension.

In recent years the discussion of Irish politics has shifted almost exclusively into the realm of culture. There is an uncritical acceptance that culture and identity are legitimate categories with which to approach the divisions within the island. According to one historian 'for all the variety of perspectives that characterise the debate, there has emerged a common view of the Irish tradition "as divided, discontinuous and founded on a problematic identity"' (G O'Tuathaigh, in E Longley (ed), *Division or Diversity: Culture in Ireland*, 1991, p54). President Mary Robinson, in many ways the symbolic representative of pluralism articulated its goal:

> There remains much to divide us. I hope that, in time, the divisions which still afflict us today will yield to a new order based on profound respect for diversity and for the rights and aspirations of others.
>
> I would like to see both traditions working towards this goal by coming to accept each other's different inheritances and by recognising the legitimacy of each other's values and beliefs. (*Division or Diversity*, p5)

Pluralism dissociates the conflict in Ireland from any political cause such as the British presence, and lays the blame instead on the failure to recognise the authenticity of different traditions or identities. It is, in spite of the hopes invested in it, an essentially sectarian view, seeing the aspirations and allegiances on either side as rooted in either a tribal or a cultural past rather than springing from the politics of the present.

The most striking thing about Irish pluralism is the way that it has crept into everyday thinking in the South. Nobody has ever subjected the values of Irish pluralism to any close scrutiny. This contrasts with the fierce debates which the doctrine has provoked in Britain and America, focusing around the questions of political correctness, ethnic culture and the values of Western civilisation. A vast literature on these subjects has built up over the years arguing for and against pluralism and cultural relativism. In Ireland, however, the concept appears to be entirely unproblematic. The words pluralism and democracy trip off the tongues of Irish politicians as if they were interchangeable concepts. But they are not. In fact, pluralism is an inherently anti-democratic idea.

The central principle of democracy is majority rule. By canvassing the opinions of a group of people on a particular proposal a majority view is obtained. The minority view, whatever its merits, is forced to submit to the will of the majority. So in Ireland, the application of the democratic principle would mean the Unionists submitting to the will of the majority, the nationalists, and accepting a united Ireland. Obversely, accepting the rights of a minority means denying the rights of the majority. In Ireland, the granting of 'rights' to the Unionists means denying the right of the nationalists to a united Ireland. The democratic principle is simple but it has never been applied in Ireland.

Pluralism strikes at the heart of democracy with the concept of diversity. According to this principle, traditions and cultures have different value systems and different beliefs, so that imposing one on the other through majority rule is a violation of their identity and their existence. Every pluralist wants to tolerate and encourage diversity. But more diversity means less freedom because people are restricted in their room for action by the need to convey respect to the 'rights' of other traditions. Where pluralism flourishes democracy and freedom die.

Pluralist rhetoric about reconciliation has assured it a liberal reputation. But that reconciliation is based on the understanding that the different identities can never be transformed. Whereas in the past sectarianism was widely regarded as something negative, something to be overcome, pluralism makes a virtue of sectarianism and celebrates its contribution to the cultural fabric. Pluralists, for example, celebrate the unique character of Unionist culture and attack republicans for their sectarianism in trying to repress it. In reality there is no such thing as a Unionist culture separate from the intimidation which accompanies it. When Loyalists parade through Catholic areas banging the Lambeg drum, they do so not for the aesthetics of percussion, but to intimidate the people of the area.

However, pluralism in Ireland also has the capacity to accommodate nationalism. Unlike the anti-republicanism which characterised Fine Gael governments in the 1970s, for example, pluralism does not seek to crush all expression of republican sentiment. In fact it positively encourages the sentiment if it is a manifestation of community spirit, but crushes it if it threatens partition. In effect, pluralism aims to transform nationalism from something which can overcome the divisions within Ireland by expelling Britain, into just another identity or tradition alongside Unionism. As such it claims to recognise the 'aspiration' for a united Ireland, and the legitimacy of the nationalist tradition, while preventing its implementation. The Major/Reynolds Downing Street declaration was a textbook case of pluralism in the recognition accorded by both governments to the 'two traditions'.

For a new idea to take hold it must also be accepted by those against whom it is directed. The evolution of the peace process indicates that pluralism has made some headway in that direction. The pluralist outlook permeated the spirit of the Hume/Adams talks, with the discussion of 'accommodating difference' and 'recognising the diverse traditions'.

It took many years for the pluralist outlook to evolve fully. We will now reconstruct the development of the idea and attempt to show the political and intellectual forces which shaped it.

The historians move in

The shift towards an acceptance of partition and a sectarian interpretation of the Irish conflict was noticeable from the early seventies within academia, and especially within the discipline of history. The fact that a new thinking directed against nationalism began in the history profession is significant in itself. It is often remarked that the Irish are obsessed with their history. This is true, though as any casual observer of British culture will note, the obsession with the Second World War shows that the British are more than a match for their neighbours across the sea on this score. What is rarely investigated is why history became so central to the integrity of Irish society after the formation of the Southern state.

Through the selective rewriting of history, the institutions of the Southern state could be presented as the achievement of an age-old struggle for freedom. But there is another dimension to it. As one writer has argued:

> History with a capital H is a representation of a national myth through a selective reordering of the past. Its objective is to develop a sense of continuity so that contemporary insecurities may be allayed by the certainties of the past. (F Füredi, *Mythical Past, Elusive Future*, 1992, p66)

Unable to provide any rationale for the present, Southern society took refuge in a constructed past in which all the fears of the present were washed away. More than most nations, Ireland lives in the past because the present is so fraught with danger. The centrality of the myth of Irish History to the integrity of society meant that the reaction against nationalism would first register in the historical imagination. Long before the demise of nationalism in politics, nationalism in history was destroyed. And the old nationalist History has given way not to a more mature, objective appreciation of the past, but to a new myth, that of sectarian or cultural History. A whole school known as 'revisionism' grew up which set about demolishing the cherished myths of nationalism. Revisionism sought to refocus public debate around the ancient sectarian character of the conflict, refusing to accept at face value the anti-British bias of nationalism.

The reaction against nationalism began in earnest in 1972. Two books appeared that year—Conor Cruise O'Brien's *States of Ireland* and Garret FitzGerald's *Towards a New Ireland*. Both suggested that Ireland was not one single nation, but consisted of two 'traditions', nationalist and Unionist. The existence of these traditions was given in history, so that any attempt to incorporate the Unionist tradition into a United Ireland was doomed to failure.

The historical character of the two traditions was further developed by the Unionist historian ATQ Stewart. In *The Narrow Ground*, published in 1977, Stewart argued that not only were the two traditions irreconcilable in their difference, but that that difference could never be overcome, only contained. Stewart's interpretation dwelt upon the irrational. Borrowing an analysis from the Swiss psychoanalyst Carl Jung, Stewart suggested that the collective folk-memory of the two traditions rendered political solutions powerless, and that attempting to 'solve' the problem only inflamed passions on both sides. For Stewart, the form and course of the conflict are determined by patterns concealed in the past rather than by those visible in the present. Thus there is no essential difference between the massacres of 1641 and the conflict which broke out in 1969. All that has happened is that the same pattern of sectarian hatred has revealed itself again. Living human beings are, for Stewart, little more than automata through which deeper sectarian urges go on asserting themselves.

Stewart's work caused quite a stir both in Britain and Ireland. Different versions of this psycho-history began to appear. Oliver MacDonagh, in his work *States of Mind*, summed up the situation in this way:

> Such a phrase as "the solution" or "a solution" to the Northern Ireland question has little meaning or promise to either [nationalist or Unionist]. They are committed too deeply to ancient roles and modes of interpreting the historical flow, and the patterns they perceive in it—or if you will, impose upon—the past, are at once a cause of the crisis, and a force making for its continuance. (1983, p14)

Here we have a case of the historical subject being a prisoner of his delusions rather than the delusions having a real existence. But the moral of the tale is the same—no escape from the patterns of the past. Thus we can already detect a key moment in the construction of a new historical myth. The old nationalists argued that the national spirit always existed, it was the pattern which revealed itself through the medium of each new generation. Stewart and MacDonagh argued that the particular pattern of the nationalists was a myth; that the real pattern was something else, sectarianism. Using an identical method, the revisionists arrive at a different conclusion.

The search for sectarian patterns leads to the rewriting of history. In order to prove the durability of sectarian identities, the divisions of the present are projected into the past. A recent example of this method is Jonathan Bardon's *A History of Ulster*. Bardon argues that the 'Ulster identity' is a product not just of the political movements of the seventeenth century, but can be discovered much further back, as far even as the Ice Age, when a line of drumlins deposited by glaciers drew a dividing line between Ulster and the rest of the country—as if the origins of the Loyalist parade are to be found in geology.

There were other sides to the revisionist critique. As well as counterposing Unionist to nationalist identity, many of the revisionists deconstructed nationalism itself. Paul Bew, David Fitzpatrick, RF Foster and the local studies school emphasised the patchwork nature of what was previously considered a unified national movement. The national struggle of 1919-23 was most commonly subjected to this method of disaggregation. Historians argued that many of those who fought against the British and against the Treaty of 1921 were pursuing narrow interests under the guise of nationalism. This is Foster on the period:

> Local studies indicate a greater degree of fragmentation (and ineffectuality) than propaganda—or memoirs—allow. Civil disruption and local feuds provided as much gratification as actual military enterprises. Many marginalised and rootless people found a *raison d'etre*; and many would cling to it by electing to fight against the Treaty in 1922. (*Modern Ireland 1600-1972*, 1988, p501)

Foster's argument is a captive of its own preconceptions. Since a local study is by its nature a study of a fragment, it seems inevitable that it will discover a great degree of fragmentation.

While it is important to acknowledge the class divisions within the nationalist movement, it is an illegitimate method to break down every political phenomenon into its diverse parts, so as to prove the political aspirations to be largely fictitious. The same method which is applied to Irish nationalism could be applied to any political institution or movement. The question for an Irish historian to answer is why the diverse elements expressed themselves politically through nationalism.

Through most of the seventies and eighties, a negative view of Irish nationalism and of the irreconcilability of the two traditions prevailed in Irish historical literature. The mood was summed up in the work of the leading Irish historian of the period, FSL Lyons. In his last book, *Culture and Anarchy in Ireland 1890-1939*, Lyons painted a grim picture. It was not politics, 'an anarchy of violence in the streets', which divided the Irish, according to Lyons:

> It was rather an anarchy in the mind and in the heart, an anarchy which forbade not just unity of territories, but also "unity of being", an anarchy that sprang from the collision within a small and intimate island of seemingly irreconcilable cultures, unable to live together or to live apart, caught inextricably in the web of their tragic history. (1979, p177)

However, from the late eighties, a noticeable shift took place in the evaluation of the nationalist tradition. This shift arose largely from the intrusion of culture into the historical debate.

The mainstream revisionists such as Stewart, MacDonagh and Foster adhered to the doctrine of the two traditions. Foster in particular argued for a more 'inclusive' definition of Irishness which could accommodate the diversity of these traditions. However the content of their analysis, directed as it was against the nationalist tradition, necessarily endowed Unionism with a moral priority. This school of historical revisionism more clearly articulated the disaggregation of the old popular nationalism than it put anything in its place.

For this reason, although they remained at the centre of academic debate, they remained on the political sidelines. To win broader support throughout Ireland, a more balanced reading of the two traditions theory, one which would grant authenticity to nationalism as well as to Unionism, was necessary. As well as endowing both traditions with historic legitimacy, a positive view of the supposed cultural division began to emerge.

The celebration of pluralism

In the mid-eighties the ideas of those who were revising the national claims of the Irish incorporated a new element into their arguments. The celebration of diversity had run all the Unionists' way in the studies of Irish historians. But celebrating diversity meant celebrating an authentic Irish culture too. The recovery of an Irish cultural identity provided the second stage of the redefinition of Irish national identity.

In the first instance, the historical revisionists were concerned to strip away the preconceptions of the old model of political nationalism. But now they were recovering a sense of national identity that would not be exclusive of the other tradition in the island, Unionism, because it would be expressed in cultural terms rather than in the universalistic political language of a united Ireland. Through the medium of a discussion about culture, the basic elements of Irish national identity were being transformed.

In Ireland the ideas of cultural diversity were taken up most notably by the cultural organisation Field Day, founded by Irish playwright Brian Friel in Derry. Set up to create a 'fifth province of the mind' where different cultures could exchange ideas, it represented that distinctive habit of the Irish middle classes of attempting to transcend division through rhetoric. Significantly, it also attracted overseas interest, with contributions from cultural critics such as Edward Said and Frederic Jameson. Unlike many previous cultural enterprises in Ireland it had a marked bias towards the nationalist tradition. One of its leading figures was the poet-critic Seamus Deane, a Derry Catholic. What would later emerge was an antipathy towards mainstream revisionism and its perceived Unionist bias.

In 1991 Field Day published a collection of essays to commemorate the 1916 Rising. In one of these essays Seamus Deane attacks Roy Foster, who has become the leading representative of mainstream revisionism. Deane's central criticism is that Foster takes a dismissive attitude to the nationalist identity.

> But what the revisionists do is to deny to the "South" the tradition that they then, perforce, accede to the "North". The "two-traditions" theory is an anomaly in historical revisionism, because it is

conceding that idea of continuity and tradition that is the bedrock of all nationalist thinking, of whatever variety. But it is, of course a *necessary* anomaly. To legitimise partition, Northern Ireland must be allowed its separate "identity", "tradition", "essence", while national-ist Ireland must have those qualities denied it. Alas, you cannot have one without the other. If Ulster is "different", its difference can be described only in contrast with the "sameness" of the rest of the island. Abandon the sameness and you abandon the difference. (*Revising the Rising*, p102)

Deane's criticism of Foster and the revisionists is that they denigrate the nationalist tradition by unfavourable comparison with Unionism. Deane is not arguing for the suppression of the Unionist tradition, but that nationalism be granted the same recognition and authenticity as Unionism.

Emphasising the uninterrogated character of Irish pluralism, Deane equates it with consumerism and calls for its rejection. If anything, plu-ralism and consumerism are opposites. Pluralism locates the individual within a given culture or tradition. Consumerism acknowledges only atomised individuals who relate solely to the market. Like Foster, Deane himself is a pluralist, except that he wants a more balanced and equi-table conception of cultural diversity in which each can embrace his own tradition without shame or ridicule. Rootedness in culture goes for historians too, according to Deane, who declares that 'history is dis-course'. This is a key theme of culturalist thinking—that the historian is so bound up in the values of his culture as to make objectivity no more than a vain pretence.

Foster rightly attacks Deane for his repudiation of objectivity (see *Paddy and Mr Punch*, 1993, pxv). But Foster takes Deane's rejection of pluralism at face value. Deane's argument is that nationalism is bound up with the Irish identity. This is the core of cultural politics—the celebration of the past and of tradition. It is also the basis for political pluralism. Foster may recoil from the consequences of Deane's argument—the worship of nationalist tradition. But that consequence is already inscribed in the logic of Foster's approach, in the doctrine of the two traditions. If Foster really wants the inclusive definition of Irishness which he claims he does, then he has to accept the nationalist tradition as part of that definition.

Other historians and critics have come to the same conclusion as Deane from other angles. JJ Lee in his book, *Ireland 1912-85*, argues that much of Ireland's difficulty arises from the destruction of its culture:

> It may be that there is an Irish emotional reality which is silenced in English. It may be too that many Irish no longer experience that emotional reality, that it has been parched out of them, that a particular stream of Irish consciousness has dried up with the decay of the language. (p668)

The notion of a unique 'Irish consciousness' is inherently exclusivist. It is also nonsensical. The Irish, like everybody else, are quite capable of engaging in the work of human culture irrespective of the language through which they have come to express themselves. To suggest that Irish is a more 'natural' language for the Irish people is absurd. Throughout human history people have changed languages without doing their psyches irreparable damage. The produce of Irish literature in the English language is testament to that.

Lee and Deane draw out the reactionary consequences of cultural history and politics. Through the affirmation of a cultural identity, nationalism is subsumed under pluralism. At the same time, the nationalist project of uniting Ireland and overcoming the divisions within the country is eliminated. Cultural identity is both a rehabilitation of the past and an acceptance of what exists.

To sum up. In the seventies and for much of the eighties, the doctrine of the two traditions had a dark, pessimistic tone, reflecting the seemingly intractable nature of the conflict in the North. In the late eighties and early nineties, with the waning of the liberation struggle and under the influence of broader trends, the doctrine changed into a celebration of the identity conferred by the two traditions. From this moment pluralism began to win a broader acceptance among the Irish middle classes because it was no longer so closely associated with an apology for Unionism. What is it about pluralism that makes it so popular among the middle classes?

The achievement of diversity

Behind the various historical and cultural debates lay a real shift in the content of Irish national sentiment. The political nationalism of the Easter Rising was turned into rhetoric by de Valera's Fianna Fail, but however perfunctorily it was meant, the constitutional claim to sovereignty over the whole of Ireland proposes a quite different sense of Irishness than the cultural identities debated by Roy Foster and Seamus Deane.

In effect the transition from a political national identity to a cultural one removes the popular dimension of the national question. A culture can serve as a collective identity for Ireland's middle classes, but in its very nature it excludes the majority. The elevation of a cultural over a political nationalism allows the reconciliation of the Southern elite with British influence in the North, at the cost of taking the fortunes of the Irish nation out of the hands of the Irish people.

The rehabilitation of the nationalist tradition is achieved by emptying it of its political content and presenting it as a cultural enterprise of the intelligentsia. The artist Robert Ballagh, a leading defender of the legacy of 1916 and of articles 2 and 3 of the constitution, represents the Easter Rising as a cultural revolution and berates today's political elite for overlooking the intellectual qualifications of its leaders:

> We hear little of Constance Markievicz's work as an artist, Willie Pearse's sculpture, or Eamonn Ceannt's involvement in traditional Irish music. We are not encouraged to examine Patrick Pearse's revolutionary work as an educator, or James Connolly's writings on social reform. (*Irish Reporter,* No2, 1991)

The purpose of such lame arguments is to expunge the central feature of the period 1912-22—the intrusion of the masses into political life. By expelling the masses from history and presenting the Easter Rising as the cultural enterprise of a self-determined intelligentsia, the most radically creative episodes in Irish history can be worked into an undifferentiated cultural identity alongside James Joyce and Irish dancing.

Today's cultural nationalism owes much to the later writings of the historian FSL Lyons. In *Culture and Anarchy in Ireland* Lyons set up an opposition between the attempts of intellectuals in the generation after Parnell at 'cultural fusion' and the cultural disintegration caused by the events of the revolutionary period. The implicit lesson taught by Lyons and assimilated by the cultural critics is that the 'rabble' should be kept out of politics. The constant use of juxtapositions in relation to Irish history and politics—culture and anarchy, division or diversity—expresses a sense of fragility and the desire to exclude the masses at all costs. The intelligentsia can realise the diversity of cultures. The mob brings only anarchy.

Looked at from another angle, the fears of the middle classes are not entirely irrational. Since the masses have no stake in the existing order, their only desire is for social transformation. But social transformation and cultural diversity are mutually exclusive. Cultural diversity rests on the notion of respect for tradition. Social transformation necessarily implies the destruction of tradition. It would be impossible to transform society while respecting what exists. Any progressive change in Ireland would require the greatest disrespect for all the traditions, both Unionist and nationalist, and the shredding of the cultural fabric.

The exclusion of the masses from politics is the precondition for the growth of pluralism, just as pluralism reinforces that exclusion. The strength of pluralism is predicated upon the political weakness of the Irish working class. The fact that the Irish middle classes could abandon traditional nationalism shows how little they take account of any other section of society. Today the middle classes discuss a new identity for the state as if a political identity was something formed in an academic discussion circle. The limitations implicit in the pluralistic conception of Ireland's national identity indicate that this is not the case.

The limits of pluralism

There are two problems associated with pluralism which make its future questionable. The first is a process of disintegration which it inevitably unleashes. As we observed, pluralism began in reality as a duality between nationalism and Unionism. However, the focus on identity leads to the formation of a genuine plurality as different groups come into existence to demand recognition for their unique identity. Since pluralism is still in its infancy, this tendency is scarcely visible.

However already in the sphere of culture the evidence is mounting that such a process is under way. In 1992, Field Day published a three-volume anthology of Irish poetry. Unfortunately for them only about a tenth of the entries were by women. The perceived marginalising of the woman's voice caused uproar and Field Day returned sheepishly to the printers to issue another anthology of women's poetry.

Irish feminism is the most vociferous of the emerging groups competing for recognition of its identity. Women's groups have shifted their attention into campaigns which demand respect for their identity. In 1992 a number of groups launched a successful campaign to have an advertisement for Falmers' jeans featuring a scantily-clad Naomi Campbell removed from the billboards in Dublin. In a country where abortion and divorce are still illegal, the obsession with images of women rather than the real conditions of existence of the mass of Irish women seems perverse. The striking thing about the Naomi Campbell case was that the old moral taboos made a reappearance under the guise of cultural respect. Despite the changes which have taken place, the elements of continuity are just as noteworthy.

The other aspect of pluralism which the Naomi Campbell case illuminated was the new role of the state in Irish society. The existence of a plurality necessarily requires an extra-cultural regulator to punish those who fail to show sufficient respect for a particular tradition. Left to their own devices, the different cultures could degenerate into an endless series of fragmented conflicts. The logic of pluralism points towards a coercive and authoritarian society where almost anything can be forbidden by the state. Relocated from the plurality within the Twenty-Six Counties into the duality of nationalism and Unionism, cultural diversity requires the authority of the British state to police relations between the two communities. Whether the immanent logic of pluralism develops in the South will depend on the movement of broader social forces. The contradiction of pluralism is that while it requires the state to stand above the cultures, it also brings it into a much closer relation with society through increasing the demand for coercion.

The other problem raised by pluralism is less ambiguous in its consequences. Pluralism can confer an identity but it can never deliver allegiance. The main weakness of pluralism is that it offers nothing to anyone. All you can do is celebrate what you are and where you come from. The future becomes no more than a continuation of the past. The key to the success of nationalism was that, despite providing nothing in the present, it held out the possibility of real change in the future. Pluralism offers nothing more than an eternal celebration of identity, of diverse forms of Irishness. It is the culture of the ghetto. Sooner or later, somebody is bound to ask, 'Is this it, is this the summit of human achievement, that we accept what we are and what exists without any possibility of change?'. Once that question is asked, then pluralism has reached its limits.

The Southern establishment's enthusiasm for Europe shows an unconscious understanding of this problem. It could be said that the affair with Europe has more to do with money than with love, but there is a political side to it too. The prospect of a European unity in which Irish identity can be incorporated and raised to a higher level offers some sort of vision. But as the centre of gravity within the European Union moves to Germany and central Europe, hopes for an exalted position for Ireland look bleak. Besides the idea of European unity inspires nobody outside of the establishment's privileged circles.

The Euro-solution shows only a vague inkling of the dangers implicit in pluralism for the Republic. Generally, the political establishment exudes a joyous disregard for the destructive consequences of the pluralist enterprise. We can perhaps illustrate the dangers by looking at what a similar enterprise would do for Britain. What would happen to the British political system if the establishment there were to slough off the symbols of British nationalism, those symbols which confer a sense of superiority over other nations and cultures? What would happen if it was to abolish the monarchy, get rid of the welfare state and repudiate its role in the Second World War by apologising to Germany for the destruction of its cities, leaving nothing more than morris dancing, maypoles and heritage theme parks? All we can surmise is that the consequences would not be happy for the establishment. The dangers for the Republic of abandoning nationalism are even greater than they would be for Britain, given the artificial and coercive character of the Southern state.

The problem of legitimacy

To appreciate the dangers for the Republic in the abandonment of nationalism we need to look at the more objective factors which expose the state's lack of legitimacy.

The first question to examine is the economic dynamism of the Republic. A country which can produce sustainable economic growth can obviate many of the problems caused by a crisis of legitimacy. Germany after the Second World War succeeded in doing just that, postponing the problems caused by defeat and collapse for nearly 50 years. Can the Republic do the same?

The economic indicators are not promising. The Southern Irish economy is one of the most depressed and most volatile in Europe. Evidence suggests that it has never been able to overcome its structural weaknesses—the lack of an industrial base and its exposure to external economic fluctuations—and is, in fact, relatively worse off now than it was before the foundation of the state. There are 300 000 people unemployed in the South of Ireland—over 20 per cent of the workforce. With fewer openings around the world for would-be emigrants, the problem is likely to get worse. Throughout the postwar period, and even into the 1980s, Ireland could export its unemployed to Britain, America and Europe. In the 1990s, an increasing number of emigrants come from the professional middle classes.

Despite occasionally strong economic growth, the structural weakness of the Irish economy has never been tackled. Following decades of autarkic policies from the 1930s, the state reversed its policy and opted to encourage foreign capital and export-oriented growth.

On the surface, the results were impressive. During the long boom from 1958 to 1973, industrial output grew by around 250 per cent. Foreign investment flooded into the Twenty-Six Counties under the conditions of the postwar boom, leading to a major shift in employment from agriculture to manufacturing. However, by the mid-seventies problems emerged which made the open-door policy look less attractive. The boom had many adverse effects. First, it laid waste to indigenous industry, already weak despite decades of state support. Second, 50 per cent of all investment in this period was state-financed, leading to an explosion in public sector debt. By the late seventies, the national debt was one and a half times GDP, and the Republic had the highest per capita debt in the world.

Most damaging of all, the frantic industrialisation of the sixties and seventies failed to create a stable capitalist class which could give some kind of coherence and direction to industrial policy. Unlike countries such as South Korea, which experienced rapid industrialisation during the same period, Southern Ireland emerged at the end of the experience somewhat wealthier, but with as little control over its economic affairs as before. Since the early eighties, the Dublin government has focused its economic hopes more on Europe than on the vagaries of international capital. The enthusiasm for Europe represents an economic climbdown from the open-door policy of the sixties. At that time, foreign capital was seen as a vehicle for industrialisation, now the focus on Europe has more to do with straightforward handouts. In effect the Twenty-Six Counties has developed a welfare economy based on the European Union's Regional Fund.

When Britain created the Free State under the partition Treaty of 1921, it handed stewardship of the South to a section of the middle classes which had up until then fought British rule. However, this section of society was very unstable, made up of disparate interest groups pulling in different directions. There was, for example, very little political or economic affinity between farmers and civil servants other than a desire to hang on to what power they had and stamp on anybody that tried to disturb the status quo. Any new opportunities presented by openings in the world economy would be exploited by these different groups for their own advantage. Hence there arose the justified reputation for patronage, graft and political and economic empires centred on individuals like former Taoiseach Charles Haughey or businessmen like Tony O'Reilly. Even though individual businessmen can achieve international success, it has little effect on the structure or resilience of the economy as a whole. Although within a given nation, capitalists will compete with each other, they will also club together at the level of the state to pursue their interests. It is the weakness of this common interest which makes the Republic so economically unstable.

Certain external factors have conspired to give the state an appearance of dynamism. Much of the enthusiasm for Europe is due to the boost it gives the country both at an economic and political level. By a quirk of geography, it has managed to avoid the fate of many third world countries with stronger economies. Not only has the EU propped up a chronically unprofitable agricultural sector through the Common Agricultural Policy, it has also financed much of the infrastructural work undertaken in the last decade. The Dublin government's sensitivity to this source of revenue was revealed when it sent foreign minister Dick Spring to Brussels in September 1993 to beg the EU not to reduce regional aid. In the event the budget was cut from £8 billion to £7.25 billion over the next five years. Despite the reduction, the Republic still gains enormously from its membership of the EU, both at an economic level, and in the prestige of being at the centre of international diplomatic and trade negotiations. In the Gatt deal struck in December 1993, two of the leading players, Ray McSharry and Peter Sutherland, were Irishmen.

Nevertheless, these external contingencies are insufficient to offset structural weaknesses within the Irish economy. The Republic's inability to create any sort of economic dynamism is evident from the social backwardness which has persisted to this day from the state's foundation.

As we have seen, remarkable social changes have taken place in the South in the last 30 years. The population of the state is increasingly concentrated in the cities, especially in Dublin. Not only that but the demographic shape of the state has changed beyond recognition. Nearly 50 per cent of the population is under 25 years of age. While the rest of Europe wonders what to do with its old people, Ireland wonders what to do with its youth.

An indication of how stagnant Southern Irish society is can be gleaned from the changing size of the workforce. In 1926 the labour force was 1 300 000. In 1986 it was 1 302 000. The static labour force was certainly not due to declining birth rates. The average Irish family is the largest in Western Europe. Rather, emigration has carried away all those who could not find employment at home. Between 1986 and 1990, 178 000 people left the Republic, nearly as high a figure as in the 1950s.

Economic decline in the rest of the world only seems to have a marginal effect on emigration levels, for the simple reason that, if the rest of the world is having problems, the Republic is having greater ones, so maintaining a balance of impoverishment between Southern Ireland and the rest of the world. The pattern of emigration has changed however. There is less emigration to Britain because of the steep economic decline in the old power. In addition, unemployment benefit is now slightly higher in the Republic than in Britain thanks to EU handouts. The pattern beginning to emerge is that the working class goes to America (most illegally) and the middle classes go to Europe and some to Britain. The increasing level of middle class emigration has sparked fears in the South of a 'brain drain' and called into question the usefulness of a higher education system which only provides professionals for the rest of the world.

Will Southern Ireland's economic decline lead to social unrest? So far the signs are that it won't. The Economist Intelligence Unit puts this down to 'the safety valve of emigration and the general weakness of the political opposition' (*Ireland to 1992*, p93).

The fragmentation of the working class since partition has paralysed oppositional politics in the Republic. The Irish working class is one of the most atomised in the West. Through most of its history under the 26-county state it has supported parties (mainly Fianna Fail) which have hardly even acknowledged its existence as a distinct section of society. Today it is politically invisible, registering its existence only as a social problem or as a thread in the cultural tapestry. The voice of the Irish working class today is the novelist Roddy Doyle. In his novels *The Commitments, The Snapper* (both turned into motion pictures), and his most recent work *Paddy Clarke Ha Ha Ha,* Doyle lovingly portrays the degradation of working class life.

Here are people who know of nothing except their own locality, with no ambition to break out of the ghetto. Yet they too have their own rich 'culture', expressed in the language of Dublin northside ('ye fuckin eejit'). Doyle's work is both an accurate picture of the grim state of the Irish working class and a middle class bemusement at the particularity of this culture which threatens nobody. The international acclaim accorded to Doyle's work (see the *New York Review of Books,* January 1994) shows that this picture of the working class is coming to be recognised elsewhere in the world.

The paralysis of the Irish working class means that the dangers inherent in pluralism could take some time to become manifest.

Without an opposition which can challenge the culture of the ghetto, the state's lack of legitimacy will not immediately become clear. The support Reynolds received when he returned to Dublin after the Joint Declaration and the widespread popularity for his Northern policy shows the degree to which pluralism and the abandonment of nationalism are passively accepted.

Ultimately the abandonment of nationalism will create insoluble problems for the Republic. As long as nationalism was the foundation of the state there was a clearly defined pattern to political life. Everybody had a fair idea what would happen if certain actions were taken by political leaders. When Britain stepped beyond the threshold of Southern Irish tolerance, everybody knew that a politician like Charles Haughey would go through the ritual expressions of outrage, assuage Irish anger, restore a sense of self-respect, and life would carry on much as before.

From now on there will be no more predictable patterns to politics in the Twenty-Six Counties. No politician in the South can have any idea what the consequences of his actions or statements will be under the pluralist regime. Without the stabilising influence of nationalism, there is now the potential for social instability in the South which never existed before. The end of nationalism will have the inevitable consequence of bringing the Republic back under more direct British control. Far from Britain relinquishing control of the North to the South, it is the South which is finally conceding its historical existence to Britain. The discussions around joint sovereignty and new all-Ireland constitutional arrangements are a ratification at the political level of something already well advanced in the military sphere. The Major/Reynolds declaration, for all its vacuity, really does mark the end of an era for the South and the beginning of something much more uncertain and unstable.

5

The North: the end of the road?

When John Major paid us a pre-Christmas visit, he talked up the promise of an economic boom if and when peace breaks out. International businessmen would come flocking in, possibly outnumbering the tourists, who would be here in droves, of course.

As he went around the city, but particularly when he was in West Belfast, he sounded like Father Christmas with his promises of jobs and investment if only Sinn Fein and the Provisional IRA would be good boys and sign up to the Downing Street declaration.

Jack Holland's Letter from Belfast, *Irish Post*, 15 January 1994

Unfortunately, John Major is no more likely than Father Christmas to bring peace and prosperity to Belfast. It is difficult to see how his Downing Street declaration might be expected to bring jobs and investment to Catholic West Belfast when it offers no change in the political structures that have enforced the impoverishment of the nationalist population of Northern Ireland since the formation of the six-county state. Indeed, by destabilising the arrangements that have been built up in the North over the past two decades of conflict, in the hope of raising his prestige at home, Major's stunt threatens to make things even worse.

Before considering the possible consequences of a settlement along the lines envisaged in the current 'peace process', let's first examine the impact of 25 years of war and successive waves of recession on society and politics in Northern Ireland.

A workhouse economy

Despite its proud record of early industrial development in textiles, engineering and shipbuilding, the North of Ireland has been in chronic decline for most of the twentieth century. The recessions of the 1970s and 1980s have devastated its residual manufacturing base, leading one account to characterise Northern Ireland as a 'workhouse economy' in which those who are not unemployed are mainly engaged in servicing and controlling each other (B Rowthorn and N Wayne, *Northern Ireland: The Political Economy of Conflict,* 1988, p98). A more recent account concludes that 'Northern Ireland does seem to be reaching the end of the road as a viable political entity' (R Munck, *The Irish Economy: Results and Prospects,* 1993, p64).

The basic features of Northern Ireland's economic decay are familiar and uncontroversial. Its historic dependence on Britain encouraged a highly specialised industrial structure, which crumbled in parallel with Britain's imperial decline, leaving the North vulnerable to the vicissitudes of the world market. In the 1960s hopes were raised of diversifying and expanding through inward investment from multinationals, but proved shortlived. According to Munck, these companies 'operated through "branch plants" which neither created linkages with the local economy nor provided a secure durable pattern of development' (p68).

In the 1970s Northern Ireland became locked into a vicious cycle of 'disinvestment, inflation, unemployment and deindustrialisation' (*The Irish Economy,* p61). The only guarantee of the economic survival of the North has been the growing expenditure of the British exchequer, which now subsidises Northern Ireland to the tune of £4 billion a year (see the *Economist,* 6 November 1993 for a detailed breakdown). Twenty years of recession have reduced the proportion of Northern Ireland's workforce engaged in industry from 42 per cent (1971) to 25 per cent (1991); the proportion in services has expanded in the same period from 47 per cent to 68 per cent. The public sector alone accounts for 40 per cent of employment and 63 per cent of GNP (compared with 47 per cent in Britain).

Looking at the same process in another way, jobs in manufacturing declined from 180 000 in 1970 to 105 000 in 1990, a fall of 42 per cent.

There are now more people out of work in Northern Ireland than working its historic mills, factories and shipyards. In 1968, at the height of the postwar boom in Northern Ireland and before the onset of the Troubles, the unemployment rate was 7.1 per cent, a level it did not reach in Britain until after the 1973 recession. In 1983, when the jobless rate in Britain topped 10 per cent, in Northern Ireland it was 21 per cent. Today, despite all the fiddling of the figures, it is rapidly heading towards that level again, and the differential with Britain remains unchanged.

Northern Ireland remains part of the United Kingdom, but by most indicators of living standards or social deprivation it is the poorest region of the UK—and generally by a substantial margin. For example, in 1989-90 average gross household weekly income in England was £329, in Northern Ireland, £233 (*Regional Trends 27,* 1992, p98). It has the lowest level of household consumer durables, such as washing machines and refrigerators, and one of the lowest rates of car ownership.

The question of the contribution of the war to the economic plight of Northern Ireland is contentious. Some economists argue, plausibly, that all the bombing and shooting and rioting have deterred foreign investors. On the other hand, the expansion of the 'security forces' in various forms has provided a substantial number of jobs. Rowthorn and Wayne have calculated that between 1970 and 1985 the war resulted in the loss of 46 000 manufacturing jobs, while creating 36 000 in 'government services'—a net loss of 10 000 (p94). Canning and his colleagues, taking a wider view of the growth of public sector employment, reckon a net gain in jobs (D Canning, B Moore and J Rhodes, 'Economic growth in Northern Ireland: problems and prospects' in P Teague (ed), *Beyond the Rhetoric: Politics, the Economy and Social Policy in Northern Ireland,* 1987, p169).

Another economist, Norman Gibson, concludes that 'both unemployment and the growth of the economy...may in actuality have been little different from what they would have been if there had been no crisis' (quoted in *The Irish Economy,* p67). There can be little disputing Munck's conclusion that 'political violence cannot be seen as the determinant cause of Northern Ireland's economic decline' (p67).

A police state

While the war may not have caused Northern Ireland's economic collapse, it has certainly made life miserable for its people, particularly in the nationalist areas. For the past two decades Northern Ireland has been under permanent military occupation, with heavily armed soldiers and police officers maintaining a constant menacing presence. All this marks the North off from other parts of the United Kingdom. People in Britain do not routinely see soldiers in full camouflage gear toting heavy machine guns and assault rifles over their garden walls and around their street corners. Nor do they see policemen and women in flak jackets and with handguns, riding around in armoured cars. They do not dive for cover if they hear a motorbike backfire or run if a strange car pulls over in the street. But this is daily life in Northern Ireland.

There have been important changes in the pattern of military rule in the North since the troops were sent in by Harold Wilson's Labour government in 1969. Troop numbers increased rapidly at first, reaching 8000 by the end of 1969 and 20 000 in 1972, the year of the most intense conflict so far. As part of the 'Ulsterisation' strategy of the late seventies, troop numbers were reduced in favour of building up 'local forces'. The Ulster Defence Regiment (UDR), formed out of the B-Specials, discredited by their role in sectarian pogroms in 1969, was boosted from less than 4000 in 1970 to twice that number in 1978. Its numbers have subsequently stabilised, but because of repeated exposures of its officers' involvement in Loyalist paramilitary terror, its name was changed to the Royal Irish Regiment in 1992. The Royal Ulster Constabulary (and the RUC Reserve) grew from a combined force of around 4000 in 1970 to reach 11 000 by 1980 and a total of 13 000 today.

Though troop numbers fell below 10 000 in 1984, they were soon increased again in response to the escalation of conflict after the Anglo-Irish agreement in 1985. There are now around 12 500 soldiers on duty in Northern Ireland, made up of six resident infantry battalions and six rotating battalions, a considerable strain on the British Army's total of 45 battalions. The overall total of armed forces in the North is now around 32 500.

The various armed forces maintain a high profile, particularly in the nationalist areas of Derry and Belfast, where the police generally only venture with an Army escort. The most familiar contact with the security forces for most people is being stopped and forced to produce some identification. Car searches and house searches are the next stage of harassment. One statistic indicates the rising scale of such events: in 1982 there were 750 000 vehicle searches, the 1992 total was 11.6m. Such contacts are always intimidating and are often accompanied by verbal abuse or physical assault. The republican weekly *An Phoblacht/Republican News* contains frequent accounts of such incidents.

The military presence goes much further than the presence of troops. Over the years, the Army has built up a highly visible infrastructure of military installations. When the troops were first deployed and their presence was regarded as a temporary expedient, they were billeted in old police barracks or army camps left over from the Second World War. These makeshift arrangements have given way to a network of extensively reconditioned or purpose-built barracks, bases and forts all over Northern Ireland. There has been an increase in the building of menacing observation towers, bristling with hi-tech listening devices and surveillance cameras, overlooking nationalist areas in Belfast, Derry and elsewhere.

The growing ingenuity of IRA attacks, using car bombs, bombs in earthmoving trucks, mortars and even helicopters has forced the British to strengthen their fortifications, with the result that large-scale concrete bunkers surrounded by complex barbed wire entanglements now disfigure every Northern town. These were described, by a conservative British commentator, as 'the most awesome and hideous urban citadels to appear in Europe since the Middle Ages' (S Jenkins, *Spectator*, 1 January 1994).

One of the most obtrusive features of the British occupation is the militarisation of the Border (*AP/RN*, 4 March 1993). This has meant the establishment of forts, checkpoints and observation towers along the Border and the closure of Border roads. Between Tyrone and Donegal, 23 roads have been closed, 26 roads between Fermanagh and Monaghan and 11 between Tyrone and Monaghan; not a single road remains open between Fermanagh and Leitrim. Such obstructions are a major inconvenience to local people and a constant focus of conflict with the occupying forces.

The prisons are another growth area in Northern Ireland, costing three times as much as equivalent provisions in England. Again in the early days, the British made do with old Army camps and even used a ship. Now the authorities have the H-Blocks at Long Kesh, one of the biggest and most sophisticated prisons in Europe—though even this proved inadequate to prevent the great escape of 38 IRA men in 1983. Before 1969 Northern Ireland had a relatively low rate of incarceration; now it has the highest in Europe, to cope with the curious 'crime wave' that followed the military invasion. Out of a total of 1900 prisoners, more than 600 are republican prisoners of war and around 400 are Loyalists. They also have a new prison at Maghaberry, specially built to take the strain off the ancient jail at Armagh, and a special interrogation centre at Castlereagh and other facilities at Crumlin Road in Belfast.

Military considerations influence every aspect of life in Northern Ireland. The new motorway system was constructed in Belfast in the 1980s with a careful eye on the sectarian geography and the need to ensure rapid access to potentially troublesome estates. Town planning in Northern Ireland is subordinate to the requirements of the security forces. Whereas in Britain, pedestrian-only zones and restricted parking areas are casually patrolled by parking wardens, in Northern Ireland the Army is in control.

A sectarian state

Ever since British troops were first deployed on the streets of Belfast and Derry in August 1969, the declared objective of the British government has been to 'bring the two communities together'. Yet after more than two decades of military rule the 'two communities' have never been further apart.

The headline story when the results of the 1991 census in Northern Ireland were published in 1993 was the dramatic rise in the proportion of Catholics to Protestants (*Irish Times*, 14 November 1993). While the population of the North remained fairly steady at just above 1.5m, the proportion of Catholics had reached more than 41 per cent and that of

Protestants had fallen below 55 per cent (to 54 per cent) for the first time ever. These reports stirred deep-rooted Protestant fears that demographic trends would inexorably put Catholics in the majority, thus destroying the historic justification for the Northern Ireland state.

In fact, speculations about abstemious Protestants being swamped by fecund Papists, which go back to the seventeenth century, owe more to prejudice than to science. Despite papal proscriptions on contraception, the Catholic birth rate and family size are in decline in Northern Ireland. Though Catholic babies have been in the majority in the North since the foundation of the six-county state, higher rates of Catholic emigration—not to mention higher rates of infant and adult mortality—have safeguarded the Protestant majority. Though there is some evidence that more Protestants are now leaving the North, some to go to university in Britain, some in search of work, most emigrants are still Catholic.

There is a grim fatalism about discussions of Northern Ireland's future that assume an inevitable direct correspondence between confessional status assigned at birth and political outlook at the time of maturity. Furthermore, nationalists who put their hopes for a better future in their superior reproductive capacities should not be in a hurry: statisticians suggest that on the most favourable estimates it could be 2025 before they are in the majority. On the other hand, others think it could take even longer, if it ever happens (O Bowcott, 'A popular misconception', *Guardian*, 13 October 1993).

The other story to emerge from a closer inspection of the 1991 census was one of growing segregation between Catholic and Protestant communities: headlines featured terms like 'apartheid' and 'ethnic cleansing' (*Independent on Sunday*, 4 July 1993). Detailed analysis of Northern Ireland's 566 district council wards revealed that about half the population live in areas more than 90 per cent Catholic or more than 90 per cent Protestant. Fewer than 110 000 people live in areas with roughly equal numbers of Catholics and Protestants. In some apparently 'mixed' wards the two communities are in fact separated by seven-metre high barriers known as 'peace lines'. Over the past 20 years the number of predominantly Catholic wards increased from 43 to 120, those almost exclusively Protestant rose from 56 to 115. In Belfast 35 out of the 51 wards are at least 90 per cent Catholic or Protestant.

The combined effects of a rising Catholic population and increasing segregation have enhanced the nationalist position in local government elections. In Belfast, the proportion of Catholics has risen from 31 per cent in 1971 to 42.5 per cent in 1991, a factor in Sinn Fein's successes in council elections in the city in May 1993. A similar pattern is evident in the rest of Northern Ireland's 26 local government areas. In 1971, Catholics were in a majority in seven; in 1991 this had risen to 11, with two more heading in the same direction.

Population shifts have created a pattern of growing Catholic predominance west of the Bann (where Catholic children outnumber Protestants by three to one) and in Derry and West Belfast. Protestants have become concentrated on the eastern seaboard, in the towns and suburbs around Belfast and in the rural heartlands of Antrim, North Armagh and North Down.

There is no mystery about the reasons for these population movements. Some people have moved in direct response to pogroms— notably in Belfast in 1969, when whole streets of Catholic houses were burned down by Loyalist mobs, and some Protestants too were driven out. Many more have moved because of their fears that such incidents might recur, or because of their fears of sectarian attack. According to one estimate between 30 000 and 60 000 people moved home in Greater Belfast in the first four years of the Troubles, 80 per cent of them Catholic (*Irish Times*, 4 August 1973). Catholic fears intensified in the mid-1970s when the notorious Shankill Butchers gang randomly kidnapped, tortured and killed 19 Catholics in Belfast. The upsurge of Loyalist terror since the late 1980s has reinforced the trend for Catholics to move into areas where they feel safe. Since the start of the Troubles approaching 900 Catholics have been victims of sectarian assassination.

Others still have moved as a result of economic factors, particularly the collapse of traditional manufacturing industry. This is the key reason for the drift of Protestants from inner-city areas like the Shankill in Belfast to the new estates on the outskirts of Belfast. Redevelopment and slum clearance have encouraged this process of migration, which has also enhanced the process of confessional segregation.

The segregation of Northern Ireland's communities has reinforced the segregation of its labour market and preserved the inherent disadvantage it confers on Catholics. Numerous surveys have confirmed that the patterns of employment—and unemployment—established over 200 years have been consolidated over the past 20. The effect of various official 'fair employment' initiatives has been to report and ratify this state of affairs rather than in any way to change it. Protestants are concentrated in manufacturing industry, in the security forces and in the higher managerial, professional and administrative occupations. Catholics are to be found in public services, though they are more likely to be nurses than doctors, teachers than administrators, in the building trade (especially at the unskilled end) and working in pubs.

Above all Catholics are likely to be out of work. A Fair Employment Commission survey in 1993 showed that the differential between unemployment for Catholic and Protestant men had narrowed: in the mid-eighties Catholic men were 2.6 times more likely than Protestants to be out of work, but by 1991 that ratio had fallen to 2.2 (*Guardian*, 26 June 1993). Over the same period the differential in female unemployment had however increased. The situation remains that Catholic male unemployment is double that of anywhere in the UK, while the rate for Protestants remains below the UK average.

Data from the 1991 census showed that 28 per cent of Catholic men were unemployed compared with 13 per cent of Protestant men (*Independent*, 5 July 1993). Furthermore male unemployment in particular Catholic areas is of catastrophic proportions, more than 50 per cent in Shantallow West (Derry), Crossmaglen (South Armagh), Creggan Central (Derry) and Ardoyne (Belfast). In Whiterock and the Falls (West Belfast) it is 58 per cent and in Brandywell (Derry) it has reached 60 per cent. Nearly 70 per cent of the long-term unemployed are Catholic.

How is this pattern of sectarian disadvantage maintained? It is important to emphasise that, once a dual labour market has become established, the need for overt discrimination recedes as informal mechanisms are enough to reproduce sectarian divisions (*The Irish Economy*, p92). Rowthorn and Wayne have summarised the main mechanisms that keep Catholics and Protestants divided at work (and keep many Catholics out).

1 Much industry is located in places which were difficult and

dangerous for Catholics to reach;

2 Catholics who sought employment were less likely to be hired;

3 Once companies acquired the reputation of not hiring Catholics, Catholics stopped bothering to apply;

4 Some trade unions acted as hiring agents and constituted a hidden but effective barrier to Catholic recruitment;

5 There was frequently no public recruitment. Employers relied upon word-of-mouth hiring through existing staff and through other social contacts.

(*Northern Ireland: The Political Economy of Conflict,* p34)

However, if these mechanisms break down and a Catholic is so presumptuous as to cross the great divide, other techniques are available. Pearse McKenna was a Catholic shop steward from Falls Road, working in the predominantly Protestant Ormeau bakery (*New Statesman,* 25 October 1991). In the summer of 1991 he complained to management about the display of Loyalist flags at the bakery, forbidden under an agreement between the bakery and the Fair Employment Commission. A few weeks later as he arrived for the night shift a man pulled up on a motorbike and fired several shots, leaving him severely wounded. Nobody from the bakery phoned his wife to tell her he had been taken to hospital.

In other cases threats are enough. In November 1993 Lisa Neeson, a Catholic from West Belfast, was awarded compensation at a fair employment tribunal for unfair dismissal following 'systematic and vicious sectarian harassment' (*AP/RN,* 11 November 1993). She was the first and only Catholic to work in the parcel office of the security firm Securicor in the Loyalist Sandy Row area of Belfast. During her first year at work, when she was 17, she received five pieces of sectarian hate mail. After suffering three and a half years of such abuse she was finally sacked.

A Catholic man was awarded compensation at a similar hearing the following month (*AP/RN,* 16 December 1993). When his job as a forklift driver at Tyrone Brick Ltd was amalgamated with a more senior position, he applied and got the job. Nearly three weeks later, his employers told him that 'a mistake' had been made, sacked him and gave the job to a Protestant with less experience. The victims of such discrimination may receive some token compensation, but they rarely, if ever, get their jobs back. Their experiences serve as a warning to Catholics to accept their position as second class citizens in Northern Ireland or face the consequences.

The inferior position of Catholics in the labour market is reflected in all the major social and economic indicators (*Independent*, 5 July 1993). More Catholics leave school without formal academic qualifications; they are more likely to live in council housing and more likely to experience overcrowding. Almost double the proportion of Catholics are dependent on social security and Catholics suffer higher levels of ill-health, with a higher rate of premature births and a lower vaccination uptake. The *1986-89 Family Expenditure Survey* found that the income of the average Protestant family was 18 per cent higher than that of Catholics, despite the fact that Catholics still tend to have larger families.

If slump and war have further polarised Northern Irish society, they have also transformed its forms of social and political organisation. The most striking consequences appear paradoxical: though Protestants retain their historic advantages, they appear a deeply insecure and troubled community; while Catholics remain the underdogs, their communities have the appearance of confidence and vitality. Let's look first at the Loyalists.

Loyalism in turmoil

The collapse of its traditional industries has been a body blow to Protestant Ulster. Firms like Harland & Wolff, whose cranes still dominate the Belfast skyline, were not just important to the Northern economy, but played a vital part in its social and political structure. Industrialists in Ulster's heavy manufacturing companies played a key role in the alliance that held the North aloof from Home Rule and consolidated the Six Counties within the United Kingdom after partition. Skilled workers also played their part in that movement, with traditions of craft exclusivity, sober respectability and patriotic deference moulded into the Orange alliance. Pride in their products, their company, their country was expressed in fierce loyalty to Crown and Empire and a combination of fear and hatred for ordinary Catholics.

In the sixties Harland & Wolff still employed more than 20 000 workers; by the late eighties it was down to 4000 and heavily dependent on government subsidies. Fearful that they would never find a private buyer, the Tories wrote off all its debts and provided another massive subsidy for a joint management-worker buyout. Total employment in shipbuilding has fallen from 12 000 in 1970 to 2400 today; in the same period the workforce in engineering declined from 11 000 to 400.

The demise of Northern manufacturing has destabilised and demoralised the Orange alliance. The once mighty Ulster bourgeoisie, which traded throughout the empire, which upheld the Union and sustained Britain through two world wars, has become dependent on government handouts. The once proud Protestant worker is no longer required at his old craft and is forced to claim the dole or take on some demeaning job in the prison service or as a private security guard, searching briefcases outside department stores. Meanwhile his professions of loyalty and his Orange rituals are treated with scarcely concealed contempt by the British.

The decline of the Shankill, the heart of proletarian Protestant Belfast, is emblematic of the crisis of Loyalism. The population of the area has fallen from 76 000 to 27 000 over the past decade, as workers have moved to the suburbs, or further afield in search of work. The Shankill has been left to rot, an expanse of boarded up shops and half-demolished terraces, populated by an ageing and embittered community with only its shabby murals to remind it of its glorious past. This is how one perceptive observer summed up the mood on the Shankill in the weeks following the IRA bomb attack on a Loyalist headquarters in the area in October 1993 which killed nine civilians:

Loss, grief, retreat—these words crop up again and again in the reflections of Protestants in West and North Belfast on what has befallen them in the last 25 years. Or the words on a wall further up the Shankill, protesting at the imminent closure of an old people's home: "Deprivation. Alienation. Humiliation. Now Evacuation."

The traumatic loss of people in the Shankill massacre is, for the wider community, a dramatic expression of a process of loss that has been slower but no less devastating. (F O'Toole, 'All change on the Shankill', *Guardian,* 1 December 1993)

The war has shattered the framework of Ulster Unionism. The suspension of the Northern parliament at Stormont and the imposition of direct rule in 1972 was the death blow to the old Unionist ruling class of landowners and industrialists. With the demise of the patrician old guard, Unionism has acquired a more petit-bourgeois and fragmented character. The squabbling ranks of Unionism are today well personified by James Molyneaux and Ian Paisley, leaders respectively of the Official and Democratic Unionists. Molyneaux, small and stiff, cautious and moderate, appeals to the respectable wing of Unionism. Paisley, big and loud, petulant and populist, attempts to hold Protestant workers within the Unionist fold.

In 1985 Molyneaux and Paisley attempted to rally their fragmented forces in the 'Ulster says no' campaign against the Anglo-Irish agreement. By introducing an 'Irish dimension'—that is, a Dublin dimension—into talks about Northern Ireland, the agreement was interpreted as signalling a British retreat from total commitment to the Union. A number of significant results followed. First, the British government under Margaret Thatcher rode roughshod over all the Unionists' protestations and refused to make any concessions on the agreement. Second, protests against the agreement led to unprecedented confrontations between Loyalists and their co-religionists in the RUC, leaving a legacy of tension and bitterness. Third, most of Loyal Ulster remained staunchly indifferent to the campaign, which gradually fizzled out, leaving the prestige of Unionism at its lowest ebb ever.

Perhaps the most important outcome of the demoralisation of the Protestant community and the disintegration of Unionism was the revival of Loyalist paramilitary groups in the late eighties. Over the years, whenever there was some sense that the Union was in jeopardy, different groups have come to the fore to express the intensity of Loyalist commitment to the Union and the depth of animosity felt towards Catholics. In 1974 when Loyalists felt that the British government might introduce some new constitutional arrangements after the Sunningdale talks, they launched a massive campaign of industrial and paramilitary action to prevent this. In the event, the British Army implicitly took their side against the government and the political initiative was abandoned.

However, by the late eighties, there was no divergence between the government and the Army. Given the demise of industry, the Loyalists were no longer in a position to mobilise industrial action against the government. Hence, the focus of paramilitary activity moved back to sectarian attacks on Catholics. There was, however, a significant difference between this and the earlier campaign. In the past Loyalist paramilitaries, working in isolation, had simply randomly targeted Catholics, following the principle expounded in the notorious Loyalist graffiti 'Any taig [Catholic] will do'. Such attacks continued, but as a result of collusion between the Loyalist paramilitaries and British intelligence services, they were also able to target known republicans for assassination. This collusion was covered up in the Stevens inquiry but exposed in the subsequent trial of British agent and UDA officer Brian Nelson in January 1992. The level of Loyalist sectarian killings increased from around 10 a year during the early 1980s to twice that level in 1988; in 1992 the number of Catholics killed was 38, in 1993 the total reached 50.

According to Jackie Redpath of the Greater Shankill Development Agency, one phrase sums up the attitude of the local community— 'siege mentality' (*Guardian*, 1 December 1993). He believes that the sense of siege at the core of the Protestant mentality has sharpened over 25 years into a retreat that is 'psychological, cultural, intellectual, political, physical and economic'. Despite the fact that most Protestants in Northern Ireland still enjoy better jobs, better living standards and a better quality of life in other ways than most Catholics, they have a deep-seated sense of resentment and grievance at the course of events over the past two decades. Whatever the facts about differentials and discrimination, there can be no doubt that many Protestants look at the relative dynamism of Catholic West Belfast and Derry, partly the result of public subsidy and investment, and consider that it is they who are being marginalised and neglected. Before we consider the likely impact of any 'settlement' on this mentality, we need to consider parallel developments in the nationalist community.

Nationalism ascendant

In the new introduction to the latest edition of his classic account of the rise of the civil rights movement in Derry, Eamonn McCann readily acknowledges the scale of Protestant deprivation in Northern Ireland. He is sensitive to the way in which 'over the course of the Troubles, they have seen their position in society grow steadily worse, not just in economic terms, but also on account of the loss of that illusory sense of involvement in the affairs of state which was once provided by the Stormont system' (p51). Furthermore, he recognises how they must resent the rise of the Catholic middle class, 'the group which won the civil rights struggle':

> The fruits of that victory are on open display, along the leafy avenues of the Malone Road in Belfast, or amid the eruption of Southfork replicas which now ruin the scenery along the banks of the Foyle, and in lush localities elsewhere where Catholic residents were an impertinent rarity 25 years ago (*War and an Irish Town,* 1993, p52).

Within the overall picture of polarisation and discrimination, it is important to recognise the expansion of a Catholic middle class in Northern Ireland. McCann documents the advance of this element, emphasising that, in Derry at least, 'in business, commerce and the professions, there's no disadvantage now in being a Catholic'. Furthermore, he notes, 'the reconciliation of these elements to the state reflects this reality'. The rise of a conservative Catholic middle class inclined towards accommodation with the framework of British rule within which it has prospered is a significant feature of the past two decades. This class has exerted a growing influence on the Catholic community and on nationalist politics.

In the absence of a highly developed political infrastructure, the middle classes in Northern Ireland tend to relate directly to quangos like the housing executive, the tourist board, the arts council and various development agencies. As former editor of the *Times* Simon Jenkins notes, 'Ulster's middle class of doctors, lawyers, professors and businessmen has shifted from democratic politics into the greater comfort of patronage' (*Spectator,* 1 January 1994). At the Northern Ireland Office junior ministers, like Richard Needham and Nicholas Scott, behave like colonial district commissioners, dispensing grants and jobs. As Jenkins describes it, 'Needham's pride and joy was the revival of Derry. He poured tens of millions of pounds of taxpayers' money into the city to bolster John Hume's SDLP against Martin McGuinness' Sinn Fein'.

By general agreement the results are impressive. Derry is humming with the sound of construction projects and the SDLP has 17 councillors to Sinn Fein's five in the Guildhall. While the Catholic middle classes luxuriate in British largesse, the historic Protestant enclave above the city walls has withered away and the beleaguered community is now confined across the Foyle in the Waterside district. As McCann observes, this spectacle is 'understandably galling to Protestants living in poverty who, just a generation ago, had been given wrongly to understand that the state was theirs' (p53).

In Catholic West Belfast, the middle class is less conspicuous and the poverty resulting from chronic mass unemployment inescapable, yet the mood of depression and despair characteristic of the Shankill is absent. While the Troubles have depopulated Protestant Belfast, they have had the opposite effect in the Catholic areas, reversing previous decline. The influx of refugees into areas like Ballymurphy in the early seventies produced overcrowding at first, but also created a closer sense of community and common purpose.

One sphere in which Catholic grievance has been at least partially redressed over the years is housing. Fintan O'Toole reports how visitors from Manchester to Springhill were astonished at the quality of the new housing. Locals pointed out that 'if they had caused as much trouble as we have they'd have nice houses too' (*Guardian,* 30 November 1993).

West Belfast has been the beneficiary of carefully targeted government spending and diverse community initiatives, often mediated through the Catholic church. For example, the Make Belfast Work scheme has spent £124m over five years in a complex network of projects, supervised by local 'Belfast Action Teams' creating 3000 new jobs (*Guardian,* 5 January 1994). The Irish Development Board claims to have 'promoted/renewed/maintained' some 4600 jobs. Many such jobs are evidently of a 'keeping idle hands out of trouble' character, and are inevitably concentrated in the Catholic areas, but they still arouse Protestant indignation.

Most significantly, Catholic West Belfast has generated what O'Toole describes as 'an extraordinary set of alternative structures', particularly where Sinn Fein is dominant:

> There is an alternative range of community organisations, an alternative language (Irish), an alternative transport system (black taxis), an alternative church (the radical community Catholicism of Father Des Wilson in Springhill), a crude alternative army/police force (the IRA). (*Guardian*, 30 November 1993)

The combined effect of such organisations is to forge, in defiance of all the deprivation and repression, a common sense of identity and purpose, which is absent elsewhere in Northern Ireland.

One expression of the spirit of the nationalist areas of Northern Ireland is the West Belfast Community Festival, which celebrated its sixth anniversary in August 1993. Reporting for the *Guardian*, novelist Ronan Bennett, himself a native of the area, noted that 'the sense that West Belfast had recovered its confidence was palpable':

> Visitors and artists saw a highly politicised, articulate and well-organised working class community ravenous for culture and appreciative of its place in real, political life. (*Guardian*, 14 August 1993)

It should be noted, however, that the celebration of a community spirit is not discouraged by the British government. It is part of the process of transforming political aspirations into cultural ones. The political consequences of the rise of the Catholic middle classes and the stabilisation of working class Catholic areas through government-sponsored projects and community organisation must be set in the wider context of the containment of the national liberation struggle. As we have seen, the influence of external and internal forces is pushing the republican movement in a more conservative and conciliatory direction. This dynamic is reinforced by the factors we have considered here, which help to foster a national movement (perhaps a 'pan-nationalist' movement) which seeks to integrate the Catholic community into the existing structures of Northern Irish society, rather than seeking to transform them.

The unsettling settlement

It is worth beginning by clarifying what any settlement would *not* achieve. It could not reverse the decline of the Northern economy or create any real jobs. Indeed if a settlement was successful in demilitarising the Six Counties, the immediate effect on employment could be drastic. According to the Unionist MP John Taylor, if there were a permanent ceasefire tomorrow, 25 000 Protestants, in various sections of the security forces, would lose their jobs (*Irish Post*, 15 January 1994). Brian Feeney, a former SDLP councillor in Belfast, suggests a figure of up to 50 000 job losses. Not much of a 'peace dividend'!

Not that any settlement currently under discussion is likely to end the military occupation, at least for the foreseeable future. The Army's latest bunkers have acquired such an air of permanence that they seem likely to last as long as the sea defences still littering Britain's east coast 50 years after the Second World War. It is ironic that discussion of an amnesty for current political prisoners continues today together with renewed demands for internment, North and South, to deal with any intransigent republicans who insist on carrying on the struggle. All the signs point to the necessity for more military force to police the settlement at least in the medium term. The announcement in early January 1994 that British soldiers' families were being moved into Army camps 'for their safety' as part of a plan 'to house all 6000 wives and children within barracks by 1997' indicated that the British authorities were anticipating neither an early cessation of violence nor a rapid departure (*Sunday Times*, 16 January 1994).

What effect would any deal have on the North's two communities? It is already apparent that the 'peace process' has had the effect of intensifying the Loyalists' siege mentality; a settlement could only intensify it further. Even though John Major may have no intention of weakening the Union, the rhetorical gestures in that direction in the Downing Street declaration are profoundly alarming to Unionists. Major's mere hints at the possibility of Irish unity under conditions never likely to be realised and his token concessions to the legitimacy of Irish national aspirations seem harmless enough in Britain; but not in Protestant Ulster. Such gestures stir fears of a British betrayal that are deeply rooted in the Protestant psyche and have been reinforced over the past 25 years.

The result is already clear. We have noted the upsurge in Loyalist paramilitary terror since the Anglo-Irish agreement, and particularly since the launch of Sinn Fein's peace process in early 1992, with the pace increasing following the announcement of the Hume/Adams initiative in 1993. Paisley's denunciation of the signatories to the Downing Street declaration, with the accusation that they had sold Ulster to 'appease the fiendish republican scum', undoubtedly echoed the sentiments of the Loyalist paramilitaries.

In the weeks before the declaration, a body calling itself the 'Combined Loyalist Military Command' had warned that Loyalist groups were preparing for 'war' in the event of what they considered an unsatisfactory outcome. On New Year's Eve 1993, the UFF issued a statement indicating its fear that the declaration threatened the Union and that it 'retained the right to respond militarily in 1994'. In the first month of 1994 there were four more sectarian killings.

Will the British be able to restrain the Loyalists? It is true that the Loyalist paramilitaries operate to a degree with the collusion of the security forces. But it is also the case that to a degree they are out of control, and in the circumstances of a general breakdown in familiar patterns, where there are a number of rival gangs all heavily armed, much blood could be spilt before order was restored. The British may well in the end put down the notorious 'Mad Dog', a paramilitary responsible for numerous murders in Belfast, but in the meantime the Catholic community has much to fear.

What about the nationalists? It is apparent that nationalist politicians are the leading protagonists of the 'peace process' and they may well be the beneficiaries of a settlement, at least in the short term. They would be involved in prestigious negotiations, and a British state keen to make the deal work would be ready with cash to promote favoured community projects. Yet in the medium term, the time scale depending on the scope of continuing instability and the intensity of conflict generated, any settlement would be likely to intensify the divergence within the nationalist community on class lines. Though Major and his colleagues may be able to win over the leaders of the SDLP and perhaps those of Sinn Fein too, they cannot provide jobs and a decent quality of life to the nationalist population of Northern Ireland. These are the questions with which the Troubles started in the first place and until they are answered, trouble will continue.

At present there is little sign of any important division in the nationalist ranks. But it can be expected that the process of incorporating middle class nationalists into the administration of some new structure in Northern Ireland will lead to a clearer separation between their attachment to nationalist culture and tradition, on the one hand, and their willingness to oppose British rule on the other. Indeed we can expect to see the emergence of a nationalist identity which is explicitly pro-imperialist—a trend already familiar in the South.

Destroying democracy

There are enough signs already that the allegiances of different sections of society are undergoing radical change. One of the most important trends to emerge in recent years is the increasing confidence of the middle classes in attempting to monopolise public debate and refocus politics around its own needs. The report of the Opsahl Commission, *A Citizens' Inquiry,* in June 1993 is one of the most significant events in the political resurgence of the middle classes, Protestant and Catholic, in Northern Ireland.

The Opsahl Commission spent over a year interviewing 'ordinary' citizens and community representatives before delivering its final verdict. According to the commission's president, Norwegian professor and UN official Torkel Opsahl, 'politics in Northern Ireland has for too long been largely dissociated from the process of day-to-day government'. The central concern of the report is how to restore 'normal' government, and take political affairs out of the hands of the paramilitaries on the one side and the unelected executive on the other.

The commission recognised that the application of the principle of majority rule within Northern Ireland could never be satisfactory since it would lead to the permanent exclusion of Catholics from political life. However, rather than concede that the state is by its nature undemocratic, the report chose to redefine the meaning of democracy. Commission member Eamonn Gallagher admitted that 'redefining democracy in a divided community as something other than majority rule brings into question the wisdom of the 1920 "settlement"' ('Northern Ireland: Towards a New Paradigm', *Fortnight*, 1994). But he did not allow his doubts to detain him.

The central problematic according to the commission was the

application to Northern Ireland of the 'paradigm of self-determination'. In the introduction to the report Opsahl observed that 'the concept of self-determination, which is the design behind so much death and destruction in the former Yugoslavia at the moment, is not a helpful one, particularly in a divided society like Northern Ireland'.

The Opsahl Report proposed the replacement of the concept of self-determination with the concept of 'parity of esteem' between the two communities. By an act of parliament, it suggested, the legitimacy of Irish nationalism should be recognised within the Northern state. As we observed in the discussion on the South, the recognition of the nationalist identity does not imply the realisation of its aims; it is simply a way of integrating nationalism into the existing order. The ordinary nationalist would still live in the same sectarian state, but would have more opportunities to celebrate the past.

So how would the redefined democracy work if majority rule was eliminated? The simple answer is that it would operate in the same way as the Opsahl Commission, through consultation. Gallagher remarks that 'the Opsahl procedure of consulting a very large number of people in Northern Ireland has discovered some points of light that political leaders can exploit in a positive way'. Put into practice, the Opsahl proposals would require the state to set up commissions to tour the state canvassing the different 'identities' on given proposals. This is no more than politics by quango. To describe it as a redefinition of democracy is a euphemism—it is the end of democracy.

Even if consultation was conducted, it would do no more than ratify the preconceptions of its commissioners. The Opsahl Report itself is a good example of this. It spent a year receiving written and verbal submissions from diverse quarters, but naturally enough, assimilated the raw data through the medium of its own prejudice—the politics of cultural identity. The commission could have saved a lot of time and energy by simply canvassing itself. It then completed the self-referential circle by recommending its own method of procedure as the basis for future procedure.

Opsahl's redefinition of democracy is in fact a negation of it. One of the benefits of democracy is that it can defend the people from the arbitrary rule of the state. At least in theory, the rulers are the object of the popular will, they derive their power from the democratic decisions of the people. Opsahl inverts that relation. Here it is the people who derive their power from the state. The British government would 'empower' nationalists through the legal recognition of nationalism, and the population as a whole through the appointment of commissions to find out what the people 'really' want. The sovereignty of the people is destroyed. They become no more than an amorphous mass waiting to be empowered by the latest batch of state-appointed experts. Opsahl is the practical implementation of the politics of cultural identity. This is its thinking: 'you, the masses, are too stupid, too locked into your own identity to be able to make rational decisions about anything. But we, the educated and intelligent don't have that problem. So we can solve things for you.'

It is significant that the politics of cultural identity have already acquired a more practical form in the North compared with the South. In the South, the absence of the working class from political life means that the consequences of pluralism and cultural identity are relatively undeveloped. In the North, however, the working class has intruded into political life in a most forceful way, if not with a strong sense of its own interests. This makes the necessity of its exclusion all the more urgent. Because it is responding to a more advanced level of conflict, the Opsahl Report is a more developed response than anything which has appeared in the South. But its attack on democracy presents a vision of the future to the rest of Ireland and even to Britain too.

The contempt for the working class is particularly marked in discussions of the IRA and Sinn Fein. The modern republican movement is frequently described as an organisation of the gutter, lacking any figures of real 'stature'. It is often unfavourably compared with the old republican movement of the 1916 period which was led by poets and intellectuals. In a particularly ill-timed contribution, Robin Wilson, editor of *Fortnight* and a leading proponent of the Opsahl Report, remarked sourly on how Sinn Fein is 'incapable of throwing up figures with whom dialogue can be meaningfully conducted....Mr Adams is hardly a Nelson Mandela or a Hanan Ashrawi' (*Fortnight*, March 1993). It soon emerged that the British government had indeed been conducting protracted and 'meaningful' dialogue with the leadership of the Sinn Fein since the middle of 1990. Adams' 48-hour visit to America in January 1994 showed that beyond the petty cliques of the Irish middle classes he is treated as a leader on a par with Mandela and certainly of higher repute than Hanan Ashrawi.

The course of the peace process shows at least who the real players are in the Northern conflict. The only group the British government is really concerned with is the republican movement. All the other players simply provide a backdrop to the real conflict between the nationalist working class and the British state. The favourite politician of the Catholic middle class, John Hume, has proved to be no more than a messenger-boy between the British and Sinn Fein.

What all sides in the current 'peace process' underestimate is the unpredictability of the consequences of any settlement. For 25 years, every aspect of life in Northern Ireland has been organised around the reality of war. Though this day-to-day reality carries a heavy cost in human suffering, it has attained a considerable degree of stability. Once the war is over, everything will be put in question—from the patterns of employment to the balance of political forces within and between the two communities. Those who imagine that there could be a return to the *status quo ante*—to Northern Ireland in 1969, with some sort of reformed Stormont—are seriously underestimating how much the world and the North have changed. Those who say anything would be better than the status quo should look at the effect of removing a stable, if repressive, framework in Yugoslavia. The people of Northern Ireland, particularly the nationalist community, are going to need all their resourcefulness for the Troubles ahead.

6

The state of the Union

The great journalist TE Utley taught me that the issue of Ulster did not merely concern its one and a half million inhabitants, nor the four million people in the Republic. It had also to do with our own sense of nationhood and the value we place on the British state. That is what we have been defending these 25 years, and that is what the IRA have been attacking. And now we seem at last to be giving up the ghost. (Stephen Glover, London *Evening Standard*, 16 December 1993)

It is rare enough that British politicians or commentators articulate the real issues at the heart of the Irish question. Glover is candid about what is really at stake in the Union and the dangers to it implicit in the Downing Street declaration. In the House of Commons the next day Tory MPs Norman Lamont and Nicholas Budgen aired similar sentiments, demanding of the prime minister that he affirm his commitment to the Union.

For 25 years the political class in Britain has been able to avoid the central issue at the heart of the Irish question. This is the integrity and unity of the United Kingdom, 'the value we place on the British state'. Behind the rhetoric about terrorists, tribalism and the rights of Unionists, Britain's tenacity in holding on to its oldest colony is rooted in the very existence of the state itself. This is the historic significance of the Irish question.

All the evidence suggests that British politicians, whether in government or opposition, know that there is more at stake in Ireland than the success of a counter-insurgency operation. Every new government as a ritual of its investiture stresses the commitment to the Union of Great Britain and Northern Ireland. In 1971 James Callaghan, who as Home Secretary in the Wilson government sent the troops into Ireland in 1969, recalled:

> We attached very great importance to reaffirming the pledge about Northern Ireland not ceasing to be part of the UK without the consent of the people of Northern Ireland. Indeed the Home Office would never present me with a draft speech or statement at that time without automatically including it by way of a preface. (J Callaghan, *A House Divided*, 1973, p175)

Sixteen years later the same formula was repeated in Article 1 of the Anglo-Irish agreement signed between Margaret Thatcher and Garret FitzGerald. The Downing Street declaration asserts that the British government will uphold the democratic wish of a majority of the people of Northern Ireland on the issue of whether they prefer to support the Union or a sovereign united Ireland. Whether Labour or Conservative, all governments have reaffirmed their commitment to the Union through the affirmation of the rights of the majority.

It is not just governments which stick to the rules. A policy of bi-partisanship between government and opposition on the Irish question has existed since the onset of the Troubles in 1969. Under this system, a tacit agreement was reached between the main parties not to make a 'political football' out of Ireland. All the parties have acknowledged that there are matters at stake in Ireland which transcend immediate party interests. As a result of this policy, Ireland is rarely discussed in parliament or in broader political circles. When it does appear on the agenda, it is to go through the ritual of condemning the IRA or passing on the nod legislation relating to the North.

Even after the introduction of internment without trial in 1971, when there was a degree of public disquiet at events in Ireland, the policy of bipartisanship never faltered. Indeed the Labour opposition went out of its way to give its blessing to this repressive measure. The *Times* congratulated Labour on its patriotism:

Mr Wilson and Mr Callaghan have ensured that the essentials of bipartisanship on Northern Ireland remain unchanged. That is a service to the nation....At moments when national responsibility is squarely upon them...Mr Wilson has never acted in such a way as to damage the political fabric of the nation, and the same is true of Mr Callaghan....Ireland is an issue on which, conceivably, the political stability of the nation could again be put at risk, as it was in the nineteenth century, when, besides nearly bringing parliamentary life to the brink of collapse, it was a deeply destructive force threatening the coherence of British society. (26 September 1971)

Though all the main parties still remain committed to the defeat of the Irish liberation movement, in the wake of the Joint Declaration a quiet note of discord was heard. It is characteristic that it should have come from the Conservative back benches, and from a Unionist angle. With the collapse of the Labour Party as a credible opposition, all political debate in Britain is now conducted inside the Conservative Party itself.

Bipartisanship is evidence of the importance the political class attaches to Ireland. Further evidence comes from the practical commitment displayed by the British ruling class to defending its rule in Ireland. No expense is spared in money or lives to the defeat of the IRA and the maintenance of the Union. Since 1984, military personnel, both Army and RUC, have increased in number from 22 500 to 32 500. Nearly 1000 members of the security forces have died since the outbreak of the war in 1969, more than in all the other combined operations of the British Army in the same period.

Since 1938 the North has been subsidised by Britain. The difference between what it pumps in and what it gets out is now around £3.5 billion a year. This figure does not include the bill from the Ministry of Defence for maintaining the British Army in Ireland. This is estimated at £477 million a year. The most striking thing is that this great fiscal crutch has never come under scrutiny or been challenged either by the opposition or within government departments. Given the miserly attitude adopted towards public spending by successive British governments it is at least surprising that the finances for Northern Ireland never seem to come under review. The money is dealt out as if there was a bottomless pot of gold sitting in the Treasury. The normal constraints on public spending don't apply to Northern Ireland. There is an illuminating anecdote relating to this in the diaries of Richard Crossman, a senior minister in the Wilson government. He recalls a cabinet discussion that took place after Wilson suggested cutting subsidies to a Belfast firm:

> It was pointed out that if we did this they would still get the subsidies from us because of the way Northern Irish finances relate to UK finances. At this point I said, "I am an ignoramus; may I be told what is the exact financial arrangement?". Nobody could say. Neither Jack Diamond [the Chief Secretary to the Treasury] nor the chancellor knew the formula according to which the Northern Ireland government gets its money. In all these years it has never been revealed to the politicians and I am longing to see whether now we shall get to the bottom of this very large, expensive secret. (RHS Crossman, *The Diaries of a Cabinet Minister,* Vol3, 1977, p187)

Judging by the sums lavished upon Northern Ireland today, the formula is still a secret.

Are we to believe that the people of Northern Ireland are so special that the British government will seemingly make any sacrifice necessary to protect them? Or is it that the government's commitment to the democratic principle is so great that it will stop at nothing to defend it?

Every word spoken by representatives of the British establishment tells us that they hold the Unionists in contempt. In fact if there is any section of the population whom they hold in regard it is the nationalists, for whom they have a grudging respect as tough opponents. The Unionists are regarded as bigots who share none of the values of a supposed British tolerance. There is a story told of how Reginald Maudling, who was Home Secretary in the Conservative government of Edward Heath, after boarding his plane to return to London from his first visit to Belfast in 1970, immediately asked for a large whisky, exclaiming 'what a God awful place that is!'. In her autobiography, Margaret Thatcher remarks:

My own instincts are profoundly Unionist. There is therefore something of a paradox in that my relations with the Unionist politicians were so uncomfortable most of the time. (M Thatcher, *The Downing Street Years*, 1993, p385)

Elsewhere she describes their patriotism as 'narrow'—presumably in contrast to hers which is broadminded. Few in Britain regard the Unionists as British. They are seen as alien in their culture and arcane in their beliefs, willing to wreck any political initiative to satisfy their own atavistic impulses. There is no reason why successive British governments should have backed them given the contempt in which they are held.

What of the argument that, irrespective of the character of the people, the majority want to remain British and therefore their wishes must be obeyed and the democratic principle upheld?

Even at the level of constitutional theory this argument makes no sense. The British polity is based on tradition, not on principle. Throughout its history the establishment has shunned any attempt to lay down a set of principles defining the limits and extent of its rule—there is no written constitution. In Britain there is not even a formal commitment to democracy as there is in France and America, for example.

The only obligation binding on the government of the day is to maintain the institutions and symbols of the state. It so happens that for most of this century there has been a system of formal democracy. But ultimate power is invested in the monarch, and he or she can dissolve parliament if the need arises.

Outside Britain itself, there is not even a commitment to democracy based on precedent. No British colony was ever ruled democratically. The people of the colonies were never consulted on who they wanted to rule over them (that went for Ireland as much as it did for Jamaica). Even if respecting the will of the majority has become the operating principle in external relations since decolonisation, it is not being applied. The people of Hong Kong have not been asked whether they want Britain or China to rule the protectorate. Whether they would prefer to join the mainland or to keep things as they are is irrelevant. Their wishes will not even be heard, let alone respected. The same thing will probably happen in Gibraltar, once again without reference to the wishes of the majority of its inhabitants.

If the government really wanted to uphold the democratic wishes of the majority in Northern Ireland, then it would revoke the Anglo-Irish agreement which Unionists hate and restore the Stormont regime (which it abolished in 1972 without consulting the Unionists). Instead it ignores their wishes and continues to enforce direct rule, a policy which accords with its own security agenda. Rarely do British statesmen explicitly repudiate the rights of Unionists. One such repudiation is a memo sent to prime minister Clement Attlee by the cabinet secretary, Norman Brook, in 1948:

> Now that Eire will shortly cease to owe any allegiance to the Crown it has become a matter of first-rate importance to this country that the North should continue to form part of His Majesty's dominions. So far as can be foreseen, it will never be to Great Britain's advantage that Northern Ireland should form part of a territory outside His Majesty's jurisdiction. Indeed, it seems unlikely that Great Britain would ever be able to agree with this, even if the people of Northern Ireland desired it. There should, therefore, be no political difficulty, as circumstances now are, in giving a binding assurance that Northern Ireland shall never be excluded from the United Kingdom without her full and free consent. (Quoted in S Cronin, *Irish Nationalism*, p235)

It is a measure of Brook's cynicism that, while he rules out any concession to the will of the majority within Northern Ireland, he adds the 'free and full consent' clause for public consumption.

The Joint Declaration states, echoing earlier remarks made by former Northern Ireland secretary Peter Brooke and the present incumbent Patrick Mayhew, that Britain has 'no selfish, strategic or economic interest in Northern Ireland'. Is there any truth to this?

What the declaration means by a 'selfish interest' is not clear. The British government certainly derives no pleasure from its continuing occupation of Northern Ireland. Every British politician would dearly wish to be rid of the place, allowing the government to run Britain proper without the trouble of a colonial war. Nobody in the British ruling class wants to stay in Ireland. In that sense, Britain has no selfish interest there.

What of the economic and strategic imperatives? As we have noted, Northern Ireland is a severe drain on the exchequer. It is a long time since Northern Ireland offered anything to the British economy. Even by the 1920s the North's economy was in terminal decline and no amount of government money has been able to revive it since. As for natural resources which might tempt the government to maintain a presence and protect its access to them, Northern Ireland has none. Far from having a pecuniary interest in Northern Ireland, a British withdrawal would boost the government's finances considerably. It would immediately knock 10 per cent off the public sector borrowing requirement.

As for strategic interests, we need to go back to Napoleonic times to find Ireland provoking any fear of an invasion which could lead to Britain's encirclement. Even in the two world wars of this century, the government was more worried about the political situation within Ireland itself than with any threat that may come from abroad, using Ireland as a stepping stone from which to attack the mainland. After the Treaty of 1921, Britain hung on to three ports in the South, Lough Swilly, Queenstown and Berehaven. A year before the outbreak of Second World War, they handed them back to the Irish Free State without impairing the war effort in any way or jeopardising British security on the Western seaboard. In an era of intercontinental ballistic missiles and rapid deployment forces, the notion of a strategic interest in Ireland looks absurd.

There is no evidence that Britain stays in Ireland for any altruistic reasons. Nor does it stay for 'selfish, strategic or economic reasons'. And yet it stays. Not only does it stay, but it becomes more deeply embroiled at every level, economic, political and military.

There seems to be an inverse relation between the intensity of the British presence and the belief in its commitment to that presence. Throughout the 25 years of war there has been a widespread belief, against all the evidence, that Britain was either looking for a way out or actually on the verge of withdrawal. This view has been most commonly expressed by those on the left of the political spectrum. Labour MPs such as Tony Benn and Ken Livingstone have declared their sympathy with the cause of a united Ireland while also arguing that Britain is ready to pull out if the opportunity presents itself. The panacea from the left is talks, so that everybody can be brought to their senses. Ironically, Sinn Fein has also clung to this view despite the evidence presented to it every day on the streets of Northern Ireland. This partly reflects wishful thinking, but more importantly it is a result of the political links between the left and the republican movement.

The left's view of the problem has reinforced two related prejudices. Firstly, it implies that Britain is a neutral player in the conflict and that its occupation of Ireland is not in its own best interests. Secondly, and as a result of this, it confirms the widely held belief that the conflict in Ireland is about two warring tribes which need Britain's selfless intervention to stop them killing each other. This latter argument has the advantage of denigrating the Irish while at the same time enhancing Britain's reputation and giving its presence in Ireland a powerful moral dimension.

The conventional explanations for Britain's presence in Ireland are both apologetic and absurd. They all ignore the historical evidence that the British ruling class attaches a political importance to the Irish question which goes far beyond immediate interest and gain. What is at stake in Ireland is the existence of the British state itself. The war in Ireland is not just a war taking place in some distant colony, but a challenge to the authority of the state within its own boundaries. It is the integrity and existence of the state itself which is under threat in Ireland.

The state is the central institution of any modern capitalist society. In the course of history, a defined geographical area emerges within which a high degree of economic, social, political and linguistic integration prevails. The historical tendency in capitalist society is for these areas to develop into nation states under the rule of the capitalist class. Through the state, the ruling class imposes its will on the rest of society. Most of the time the rule of the state goes unchallenged and there is a degree of consent to its authority. In the case of Britain there has been historically a high degree of acquiescence to the authority of the state. However, even in Britain the ultimate guarantor of social stability and capitalist rule is force, imposed by the police and army.

Without a state apparatus respected by most of society, the capitalist class could not rule. If consent is withdrawn within any section of the political boundaries defined by the state, then the entire organism is disturbed. Only in the most extreme circumstances will the state allow its boundaries to be redefined. This generally happens only as a result of war where the vanquished power is forced by the victor to cede a portion of its territory. Such an event leads almost inevitably to a severe crisis of authority within the vanquished state itself since its prestige and legitimacy have been grievously undermined in the eyes of its own citizens.

Yet we are presented with a paradox here. The state is the central institution of capitalist society. But it is rarely discussed, and as the case of Ireland illustrates, the integrity of the state is widely considered to be of minor import. Only since the onset of the peace process has the broader question of the unity of the United Kingdom come to the surface of public debate.

It would be wrong to suggest that the real interests of the state which Britain is defending in Ireland are consciously suppressed by the establishment. That is not to say that the British establishment would never conspire against its opponents or against the people of Britain. In fact the British cabinet is a sitting conspiracy against all the citizens of the state (its deliberations are only revealed 30 years after the event, if we're lucky). However despite its best efforts, it cannot completely control public debate.

One of the peculiarities of the British political system is that the state as an institution is rarely subjected to any close scrutiny. State spending may cause soul-searching debate about the prospects for the British economy, but the question of the state itself, rather than what it does, seldom enters the political arena. It is striking that the phrase 'the British state' is rarely used in political discourse. Euphemisms such as 'Her Majesty's Government', the United Kingdom or 'the realm' are used to refer to the state. This contrasts with the Irish Republic where phrases such as 'the defence of the state' are common currency.

The unquestioning attitude towards the state in British politics reflects above all the extraordinary political stability and continuity of the institutions of the British ruling class. This stability and continuity arises out of Britain's position as the world's first capitalist power and later as the world's first global superpower. It should be noted that the only other state in the world to have achieved comparable levels of stability is the only other global superpower in history—the United States.

There has never been a general and open social war between the main classes of British society. We have to go back to the English Civil War of the 1640s to find anything resembling an open social conflict. Even then, the classes themselves were so ill-defined and the language and ideas of the conflict so dressed up in the garb of religious millenarianism that its social roots are well obscured. The 'Glorious Revolution' of 1688 settled conflicts within the ruling class with a power-sharing agreement which avoided open class war between different sections of society.

In the modern period, the working class, which in the nineteenth century was larger and more highly organised than any other in western Europe, was nevertheless successfully integrated into British society through the agency of the state and the labour bureaucracy in the form of the trade unions and later of the Labour Party. At no time did the working class become sufficiently conscious of itself and its distinct interests to pose a challenge to capitalist rule. As a result, the state and all the other institutions of British society were never shaken to their foundations in a way that happened in Europe.

By way of contrast, take Britain's nearest European neighbour, France. In 1789 the French bourgeoisie overthrew the aristocracy in a revolution which escalated in violence and terror until it shook all of Europe and left an indelible mark on world politics. In 1830 and again in 1848, France was racked by revolutionary violence. In 1871 the French state collapsed following war with the newly united Germany and the world's first proletarian regime took power in the Paris Commune. The Commune was brutally suppressed and the Republic re-established. In the twentieth century the Republic collapsed twice, in 1940, again following a German invasion, and in 1958 as a result of the colonial war in Algeria. In 1968 the Fifth

Republic survived the civil disorder caused by student rebellion and a general strike. Two hundred years of bitter international and class conflict have left a deep scar on the consciousness of the French ruling class and made them acutely sensitive to the fragility of power.

It is over 900 years since Britain was invaded and 300 years of relative social peace have given an almost mystical aura to the continuity of political institutions. As a result, the state appears in Britain as a spontaneous and eternal entity, independent of the social and political forces from which it sprang. That is why the political class rarely talks about the state; since it is assumed to be a given, there is little point in talking about it.

Only in rare moments of crisis do the state and the Union become a subject for debate. The last time that happened in Britain was in the years leading up to the First World War, in the course of the violent controversy surrounding the third Home Rule Bill. In her autobiography, Margaret Thatcher recalls:

> Our party has always, throughout its history, been committed to the defence of the Union: indeed on the eve of the First World War the Conservatives were not far short of provoking civil disorder to support it. (*The Downing Street Years*, p385)

On the eve of the First World War, the British establishment was undergoing the greatest internal crisis in its modern history. Britain's pre-eminence as the world's leading power was being challenged by new imperial powers, mainly the United States and Germany. The Great Depression from 1873 to 1896 affected Britain alone, since it was the only capitalist power to have reached a sufficient level of maturity. As a result, British industry failed to keep up with its rivals. From the 1890s, the doctrine of free trade, which had been the cornerstone of British economic policy for most of the century, was coming under sustained attack from groups calling for the imposition of tariffs and the granting of preferential trading rights to the rest of the empire. 'The weary titan staggers under the too-vast orb of its fate', declared leading tariff reformer Joseph Chamberlain, before going on to call on the (white) colonies to come to the aid of the mother country.

The period up to the First World War was also characterised by a high level of class conflict and, almost unique in British history, the formation of working class organisations independently of the labour bureaucracy. At the same time, the militant campaign for women's suffrage traumatised the British establishment.

It was around the Irish question that the battle lines were drawn between those in favour of a more laissez-faire policy in politics and economics, and those in favour of a full-blooded imperial policy. Successive Liberal administrations had put forward proposals for Irish Home Rule. The first two bills were defeated by the House of Lords, which as the chamber representing the aristocracy had most to lose from a weakening of the link with Ireland given its extensive landed interests there. However, on the third Home Rule Bill, the Conservative Party united with sections of the Liberal Party and the Ulster Unionists to oppose Home Rule.

Large sections of the British establishment were prepared for civil war against Asquith's Liberal administration rather than concede Home Rule. They perceived, quite correctly, that at a time when the British Empire was in such difficulties both at home and abroad, tampering with the state was little short of treason. Conceding Home Rule would be a signal to the world that Britain could not even preserve the integrity of its own state.

Andrew Bonar Law, the Conservative leader, scoffed at the sovereignty of parliament and its assent to Home Rule, declaring that 'there are things greater than parliamentary majorities'. The distinguished constitutional theorist, AV Dicey, warned 'moral resistance...will, from a constitutional point of view, be fully justified. I do not even assert that it may not rightly be carried by Ulstermen to extreme lengths' (quoted in F Mount, *The British Constitution Now*, 1992, p55). In March 1914, the Army garrison stationed at the Curragh Camp in Ireland mutinied in anticipation of being asked to enforce Home Rule. One historian remarks: 'that His Majesty's government, for the first time since the revolution of 1688, had lost the allegiance of His Majesty's forces; that it was powerless.' (G Dangerfield, *The Strange Death of Liberal England*, 1970, p304). Only the outbreak of the First World War prevented the Home Rule crisis from erupting into full-scale civil war.

The Tory Party became the Conservative and Unionist Party and was transformed into the natural party of government by its staunch defence of the Union. The years leading up to 1914 were the last occasion when the Irish question seriously disturbed British politics. They were also the last occasion that the crucial issues of the integrity and legitimacy of the state came to the surface of political life.

It takes a severe crisis to bring the problem of the state to the surface. In the normal run of things, British statesmen just get on with the job of running the machine without questioning publicly the motives and aims of the Union over which they preside. It is only when Conservative politicians are pushed willy-nilly to the margins of political life that they become sensitive to the importance of the Union. Following the collapse of the Thatcher administration in 1990, and the difficulties which have beset the Major one, there is a rich crop of disaffected backbenchers. Norman Lamont, Cecil Parkinson, Norman Tebbit and Margaret Thatcher herself have all expressed disquiet at the course of the peace process and the Joint Declaration. Traditionally it is such mavericks who have articulated most coherently the principles which are under attack and which the British are defending in Ireland. Enoch Powell is perhaps the classic representative of this group. Once a leading member of the Conservative Party and a former Unionist MP, he has sensed the principles at stake in Ireland:

> Ulster is Britain's test of its own will to be a nation. A nation that will not defend its own frontiers or recognise the rights of its own people is well on the way to being no nation. (*Guardian,* 15 February 1980)

The problem that Ireland presents to Britain is that within the frontiers of the state there is a population which does not accept the authority of the state. Even if Irish nationalism is no longer the force it was, the artificial and coercive character of the Union will continue to generate instability and disaffection. Like most things, the state is only as strong as its weakest point. There is no political solution which can overcome these weaknesses and make Northern Ireland a normal part of the United Kingdom. Consequently, the only reliable way of compensating for the inherent weaknesses in the Union of Great Britain and Northern Ireland is military force.

Whether it likes it or not, the British ruling class is stuck with Ireland. The original Act of Union in 1801 which brought Ireland within the frontiers of the British state proper simply transformed a colonial problem into a domestic one. But the problems which Britain faced in the late eighteenth century and which the Union temporarily solved do not exist today. Instead a whole new set of difficulties has been thrown up to which the British establishment is constantly forced to come up with new solutions. The Union seemed a good solution at the time (after all Scotland had been successfully integrated in 1707). However, once made, it could not be unmade without causing serious damage to the state as a whole. The British ruling class is still dealing with the legacy of the battles it fought nearly 200 years ago.

Integrating a colony into the body politic of the metropolitan power is inherently dangerous for the coloniser. It exposes the colonising power to the full blast of rebellion and can stimulate discontent in the rest of society. Other colonial struggles illustrate the dangers of such a strategy. Algeria's links with France bore some resemblance to Anglo-Irish relations, since France claimed Algeria as part of the French state proper. Consequently, when a war of independence broke out in Algeria in 1956, it immediately polarised French society around the question of the state. The war resulted in a military coup led by Charles de Gaulle, the collapse of the Fourth Republic and widespread unrest. In October 1961, 200 Algerians were massacred by police in the streets of Paris. Similarly, the defeat of the Portuguese in Angola and Mozambique in 1974 led to the overthrow of the Caetano regime in Lisbon the following year and a prolonged period of class conflict. However, neither France nor Portugal had as close a relationship with their colonies as Britain has with Ireland. There is an intimacy of historical and political bonds between Britain and Ireland which is unique in the world and impossible to unravel.

There are two possible responses to the challenge posed by integration. One is to affirm the Union and reinforce it. The other is to isolate the discontent as far as possible within the limits set by the

Union. Britain has deployed both strategies in its Irish policy with a high degree of success.

The partition of Ireland in 1921 strengthened the bond which had previously existed with the whole of Ireland by concentrating it on the North. At the same time, the creation of the Stormont and Dublin regimes removed the Irish question from British politics, a welcome respite for Britain given the turmoil it had caused in the preceding years. In his 1918 election manifesto, Lloyd George pointed out that so long as the Irish question remained unsettled, there could be 'no political peace either in the United Kingdom or in the Empire'. By that time a consensus had emerged within the British establishment as a whole that the near calamity of the prewar years must be avoided at all costs. The dismemberment of Ireland was seen as the perfect solution.

For 50 years partition proved remarkably successful in isolating the Irish problem. It removed virtually all business relating to Ireland from politics at Westminster and left the Unionists to run the North as their private fiefdom. Even though Northern Ireland was an integral part of the United Kingdom, it may as well have been on the other side of the planet.

The outbreak of war in 1969 threatened to bring this carefully constructed arrangement crashing down. The early years of the war were characterised by a certain amount of panic on London's part at the prospect of Ireland once again disrupting political life in Britain. The suspension of Stormont and the imposition of direct rule in 1972 meant the abandonment of an arrangement that had prevailed for half a century, a serious setback to British authority. However, the absence of any dissenting voices within Britain to Irish policy and the relative containment of the military threat from the IRA gave the government the scope to 'Ulsterise' the conflict, remove the Army as much as possible from the front line and confine the conflict to Northern Ireland itself.

The two-fold strategy of integration and isolation, however, can never be entirely satisfactory. In fact it builds up new problems which may lie dormant for a long time, but which sooner or later will come to the surface.

The central problem is that it creates a differentiation within the state itself, undermining the very Union which it is intended to secure. Isolating Northern Ireland within the Union implies that there are in fact two distinct states, Britain and Northern Ireland. In fact if we look at it more closely, this differentiation exists in the constitutional arrangement between the two parts of the United Kingdom. The Northern Ireland Act of 1949 states that:

> In no event will Northern Ireland or any part thereof cease to be part of His Majesty's dominions and of the United Kingdom without the consent of the parliament of Northern Ireland.

In order to give legitimacy to its continued rule over Northern Ireland, the British ruling class introduced a bogus democratic principle into the constitutional relation between the two parts of the United Kingdom. But as we have observed, this democratic principle does not operate in Britain proper. There, Her Majesty rules whether you like it or not. Hence, from the beginning there was an element of contingency introduced into the unity of the state. Unlike the British, the people of Northern Ireland can, ostensibly, opt out of the Union.

The underlying contingency of the state in the Six Counties does not reveal itself as a problem for as long as the government states its commitment to the Union. But when the principle of consent is pushed a step further, and the government feigns indifference as to the outcome of the democratic wishes of the people of Northern Ireland, then the alarm bells start ringing. This is the fatal flaw at the heart of the Joint Declaration.

The reservations expressed about the declaration by senior figures within the establishment now sound more plausible. According to Sir David Goodall, a key official in the 1985 Anglo-Irish agreement:

> The tone of the declaration moves the British government a shade further towards accepting a united Ireland as an attainable rather than simply a conceivable goal. (*The Tablet*, 25 December 1993)

The editor of the *Sunday Telegraph* was even more disturbed by the tone of the declaration:

The implication is that, since the British government has no "self-ish" interest, it has no commitment to the Britishness of Northern Ireland....Nowhere in the declaration does the British government support the integrity of the state that it governs. (2 January 1994)

When the Conservative MP for Wolverhampton, Nicholas Budgen, asked John Major in the commons, the day after the declaration, whether the government still had 'a selfish, strategic or economic interest in Wolverhampton', he touched on the heart of the matter. There are many parts of the United Kingdom which, from an administrative point of view, the government would be just as happy to be rid of. Merseyside immediately springs to mind, possibly Wolverhampton too. But the point about the state is not the character of the areas over which it governs, but the principle of its right and authority to rule the territory over which it claims jurisdiction. It is a point of principle, not of place. If the state is willing to cede control in Irish territories that have been part of the United Kingdom since the beginning of the nineteenth century, then the future of the entire state is immediately put in jeopardy. The state is not divisible. Only the most narrow-minded administrator would fail to realise the implications for the rest of the apparatus of disengaging from a part.

The threat to the Union implicit in the Joint Declaration is compounded by the international framework within which this initiative has taken place. It is now widely recognised that the end of the Cold War has left the institutions of the Western world in tatters. Without the stability provided by the framework of the Cold War, the institutions of Western society seem makeshift and lacking in inspiration. In Britain, the monarchy is ridiculed, the political parties are held in disdain, and the judiciary treated with suspicion.

It was the decline of the political institutions of the ruling class, manifested particularly in the plunging prestige of his government, which tempted Major to be bold and agree to the Joint Declaration. Set against the prospect of being known as the man who brought peace to Ireland, all the misfortunes of his government would fade into the background.

The Joint Declaration and the peace process could yet be his undoing. And not just Major's. Greater matters than the success or failure of the present government are at stake in Ireland. Tampering with the state at any time is dangerous. Tampering with it when it is in such a poor condition could bring down more than a government.

The Downing Street declaration is symptomatic of a much deeper malaise afflicting the British establishment in the 1990s. For the first time in its modern history, the establishment has no broad strategic objectives within which to manage its diverse affairs. At every stage in the past 200 years, the ruling class was united around the pursuit of some clearly defined aims. In the nineteenth century, the expansion of British capitalism led to the development of a global network of trading relations which was later consolidated into a vast empire which ringed the globe. The maintenance of a balance of power in Europe through a carefully managed system of alliances was the strategic imperative for the success of free trade and the later growth of Empire. In the twentieth century the challenge of rival imperialist powers forced the ruling class to pull together and develop a strategy which balanced the demands of Empire with the growing might of the United States and Germany. After the Second World War, those conflicting demands were managed effectively within the stable framework of the Cold War.

The inexorable decline of the British economy and the disappearance of all the old patterns which shaped international affairs have left the ruling class bereft of any clear vision of the future or strategic priority. The disappearance of all its traditional foes such as the Soviet Union and the labour movement has compounded the loss of purpose and eroded the old sense of class solidarity.

The result of this loss of direction is that the British ruling class is now doing things which seem quite out of character. The British establishment was once renowned for its cautious, calculating and cut-throat diplomacy, a diplomacy which contrasted with the erratic and volatile behaviour of its European rivals. The cautious character of British diplomacy reflected the fact that it was an established power with extensive commitments around the world and was therefore forced to play a game of stealth and cunning with its rivals.

Britain's decline and the loss of any broad strategic framework mean that the ruling class now seems to consider only short-term considerations—such as how to make the government more popular. This is a dangerous position for the ruling class. It disposes it to the pursuit of policies the consequences of which are not clearly defined, indeed cannot be defined because there is no longer any clear long-term goal.

The effects are most obvious in domestic politics. The ill-fated 'Back to basics' policy inaugurated by John Major at the Conservative Party conference in 1993 was launched to give the impression that the Conservatives had a clearly defined set of moral principles. But given the incoherence of the ruling class and the new zeal with which the media go about exposing the sexual proclivities of the rich and famous, it is little surprise that it was the Conservative Party itself which first came under moral scrutiny.

The Downing Street declaration is just another government initiative which aims to secure short-term gain from diplomatic triumph. But this is no ordinary political initiative. The declaration makes the state itself the centre of political negotiation. In order to secure the defeat of the republican movement and a victory for the Major government, key political principles which have been sacrosanct for 25 years and more have been put to one side. Overnight, the criminal status attached to Irish republicanism has been dropped and the government has officially declared its indifference towards the future shape and constitution of the British state. Such radical and dangerous initiatives for the ruling class are bound to have repercussions which go far beyond the immediate circumstances within which the declaration was framed. Britain's new Irish policy has unleashed a process which could take it into new, uncharted waters where almost anything can happen.

It may take some time before the consequences of the Joint Declaration and the new political map in Britain and Ireland come clearly into focus. The lack of any dynamic within British politics will retard developments and the war may continue at a declining level for some years. Rather than becoming a focus for discontent, Tory disquiet at the declaration could subside.

At an intellectual level, the ruling class is exhausted. The sense of resignation expressed by Stephen Glover, that 'we seem at last to be giving up the ghost', is widely held within the political establishment.

This sense of resignation has also extended to the nation state. In 1993, popular historian Paul Kennedy published a bestseller, *Preparing for the Twenty-First Century,* a nightmare vision of the future. It painted the familiar picture of a world struggling with overpopulation, beset by famine, attempting to cope with ecological devastation and terrorised by Islamic fundamentalists. One of the more positive notes he struck was on the future of the nation state. It had none. According to Kennedy, with the globalisation of capital and the growth of regional political identities, there would be no place for the old nation state in the next century.

For the ruling class, this is the ultimate nightmare. If it has no belief in the future of the nation state then it has no belief in its own ability to control or change the course of events, since that is the agency through which it exerts its power.

Given the malaise that currently grips the British establishment, it is conceivable that it believes that withdrawal from Ireland is possible, that the state no longer matters. But the practical consequences of such actions, should the establishment attempt them, would soon wake it from its reverie. The ruling class would soon find more than Ireland slipping from its grip.

Whatever the outcome of the deliberations within the ruling class on the Joint Declaration, one thing is certain. Anglo-Irish relations will never be the same again. All the old pointers which gave meaning to the Irish question are gone for good. Traditional Irish nationalism is dead, the future of Loyalism is uncertain and the British establishment is exhausted and divided. Anglo-Irish relations are entering a new phase which is likely to prove violent and unstable. A chapter has closed in the Irish question. A new one is about to begin.

Bibliography

Books

Adams, Gerry, *The Politics of Irish Freedom*, Brandon Books, Dingle, Kerry, 1986

Bardon, Jonathan, *A History of Ulster*, Blackstaff Press, Belfast, 1992

Beloff, Max, *Imperial Sunset*, Methuen, London, 1969

Berresford Ellis, Peter, *The Making of the Irish Working Class*, Pluto, London, 1985

Bew, Paul and Patterson, Henry, *The British State and the Ulster Crisis: From Wilson to Thatcher*, Verso, London, 1985

Bowyer Bell, J, *The Secret Army: The IRA 1916-79*, Academy Press, Dublin, 1979

Cahill, Liam, *Forgotten Revolution: Limerick Soviet 1919, a Threat to British Power in Ireland*, O'Brien Press, Dublin, 1990

Callaghan, James, *A House Divided: The Dilemma of Northern Ireland*, Collins, London, 1973

Connolly, James, *Labour, Nationality and Religion*, Dublin, 1969

Cronin, Sean, *Irish Nationalism: A History of Its Roots and Ideology*, Academy Press, Dublin, 1980

Crossman, RHS, *The Diaries of a Cabinet Minister*, Hamish Hamilton and Jonathan Cape, London, 1977

Cruise O'Brien, Conor, *States of Ireland*, Hutchinson, London, 1972

Dangerfield, George, *The Strange Death of Liberal England*, Paladin, London, 1970

Devlin, Bernadette, *The Price of My Soul*, Pan Books, London, 1969

Doyle, Roddy, *Paddy Clarke Ha Ha Ha,* Secker & Warburg, London, 1993

Field Day, *Anthology of Irish Poetry,* Field Day, 1992

Fitzgerald, Garret, *Towards a New Ireland,* Charles Knight, London, 1972

Foster, RF, *Modern Ireland 1600-1972,* Penguin Books, Harmondsworth, 1988

Foster, RF, *Paddy and Mr Punch: Connections in Irish and English History,* A Lane, London, 1993

Freeman, Mike, *The Empire Strikes Back: Why We Need a New Anti-War Movement,* Junius, London, 1993

Füredi, Frank, *Mythical Past, Elusive Future: An Essay in the Sociology of History,* Pluto Press, London, 1992

Gallagher, E and Worrall, S, *Christians in Ulster 1968-80,* Oxford University Press, Oxford, 1982

Gaughan, JA, *Austin Stack: Portrait of a Separatist,* Kingdom Books, Dublin, 1977

Gilmore, George, *The Irish Republican Congress,* Cork Workers Club, Cork, 1978

Greaves, C Desmond, *Liam Mellows and the Irish Revolution,* Lawrence & Wishart, London, 1971

Greaves, C Desmond, *The Life and Times of James Connolly,* Lawrence & Wishart, London, 1976

Hamill, Desmond, *Pig in the Middle: The Army in Northern Ireland 1969-84,* Methuen, London, 1985

Hussey, Gemma, *Ireland Today: Anatomy of a Changing State,* Viking, London, 1993

Jones, Tom, *Whitehall Diary: Volume III, Ireland 1918-25,* Oxford University Press, Oxford, 1971

Kelley, Kevin, *The Longest War: Northern Ireland and the IRA,* Zed Press, London, 1982

Kennedy, Paul, *Preparing for the Twenty-First Century,* Harper Collins, London, 1993

Lee, JJ, *Ireland 1912-85: Government and Society,* Cambridge University Press, Cambridge, 1988

Longley, Edna (Ed), *Division or Diversity: Culture in Ireland,* Queen's University Institute of Irish Studies, Belfast, 1991

Lyons, FSL, *Culture and Anarchy in Ireland 1890-1939*, Oxford University Press, Oxford, 1979

MacDonagh, Oliver, *States of Mind: Two Centuries of Anglo-Irish Conflict 1780-1980*, Century, London, 1983

MacStiofain, Sean, *Memoirs of a Revolutionary*, Gordon Cremonesi, London, 1975

McCann, Eamonn, *War and an Irish Town*, Pluto Press, London, 1993

Milotte, Mike, *Communism in Modern Ireland: The Pursuit of the Workers' Republic since 1916*, Gill & Macmillan, Dublin, 1984

Mount, Ferdinand, *The British Constitution Now: Recovery or Decline*, Heinemann, London, 1992

Munck, Ronnie, *The Irish Economy: Results and Prospects*, Pluto Press, London, 1993

Ni Dhonnchadha, Mairin and Dorgan, Theo (Eds), *Revising the Rising*, Field Day, 1991

O'Brady, Rory, *Our People, Our Future: What 'Eire Nua' Means*, Sinn Fein, Dublin, 1973

The Opsahl Report: A Citizens' Inquiry, Lilliput, 1993

Rowthorn, Bob and Wayne, Naomi, *Northern Ireland: The Political Economy of Conflict*, Polity Press, Cambridge, 1988

Sinn Fein, *The Politics of Revolution: Main speeches and Debates from the 1986 Ard Fheis*, Sinn Fein, Dublin, 1986

Stewart, ATQ, *The Narrow Ground: The Roots of Conflict in Ulster*, Faber & Faber, London, 1977

Teague, Paul (Ed), *Beyond the Rhetoric: Politics, the Economy and Social Policy in Northern Ireland*, Lawrence & Wishart, London, 1987

Thatcher, Margaret, *The Downing Street Years*, Harper Collins, London, 1993

Magazines, periodicals

An Phoblacht/Republican News, Dublin and Belfast
Economist, London
Fortnight, Belfast
HMSO: Regional Trends, London
HMSO: Family Expenditure Survey, London
Irish Reporter, Dublin
Labour Briefing, London
Living Marxism, London
London Review of Books, London
New Left Review, London
New Statesman and Society, London
New York Review of Books, New York
Spectator, London
The Tablet, London
Workers Press, London

Index

167

INDEX

Published by Pluto Press

War and an Irish Town

Eamonn McCann

'There is no denying the powerful ways in which McCann recounts the events of those early years of the troubles ...'
Robert Fisk, *The Times*

'Few could quarrel with the publisher's description of this as a classic.'
Books Ireland

ISBN paperback 0 7453 0725 6

Suspect Community

People's Experience of the Prevention of Terrorism Act in Britain

Paddy Hillyard

The first independent research into people's experience of the operation of the Prevention of Terrorism Acts, together with a systematic analysis of the impact the legislation has on Great Britain. Published in association with Liberty

ISBN hardback: 0 7453 0727 2 softback: 0 7453 0726 4

Order from your local bookseller or contact the publisher on 081 348 2724.

Pluto Press
345 Archway Road, London N6 5AA
5500 Central Avenue, Boulder, Colorado 80301, USA

Published by Pluto Press

Legion of the Rearguard
The IRA and the Modern Irish State

Conor Foley

'A good detailed account of the activities of militant
republicans in the Twenties and Thirties, both north and
south of the border . . . a timely and useful work.'
Irish Times

ISBN hardback: 0 7453 0685 3   softback: 0 7453 0686 1

Justice Under Fire
The Abuse of Civil Liberties in Northern Ireland

Edited by Anthony Jennings

ISBN hardback: 0 7453 0263 7 softback: 0 7453 0415 X

Labour and Partition
The Belfast Working Class 1905–1923

Austen Morgan

ISBN hardback: 0 7453 0326 9   softback: 0 7453 0588 1

Order from your local bookseller or contact the publisher on
081 348 2724.

Pluto Press
345 Archway Road, London N6 5AA
5500 Central Avenue, Boulder, Colorado 80301, USA

Published by Pluto Press

The Irish Economy

Ronnie Munck

The economy of Northern Ireland is usually considered as part of the United Kingdom. But Ronnie Munck argues that, with the single European market, it no longer makes sense to consider the economies of the North and South separately and that the real situation can only be understood in terms of the history of the Irish economy as a whole.

This is the only book to provide a broad historical overview of both the Republic and Northern Ireland and to consider possible alternatives to the present situation. In his controversial conclusion, Munck argues that although we might expect some significant improvements in the economy with Irish unification, the underlying problems would remain: only functional social and political transformation can achieve a democratically accountable economy.

ISBN hardback: 0 7453 0673 X softback: 0 7453 0674 8

Order from your local bookseller or contact the publisher on
081 348 2724.

Pluto Press
345 Archway Road, London N6 5AA
5500 Central Avenue, Boulder, Colorado 80301, USA